Basic Artificial
Intelligence Skills

Dr. Prasun Bhattacharjee

DEDICATION

To the luminaries who have illuminated my path, this work,
"Basic Artificial Intelligence Skills", is humbly offered:

To Dr. Somenath Bhattacharya,
A scholar par excellence, whose profound guidance and
nurturing mentorship have been the cornerstone of my
academic pursuits, inspiring me to dream beyond horizons
and delve into the depths of innovation.

To Dr. Rabin K. Jana,
A visionary and guide, whose sharp intellect and unyielding
support have ignited my curiosity and sharpened my resolve
to strive for excellence in every endeavor.

To Swami Umapadananda ji Maharaj,
A spiritual lighthouse, whose serene wisdom and
compassionate presence have imbued my journey with
purpose, reminding me always of the higher ideals of service,
humility, and devotion.

With heartfelt gratitude, I dedicate this book to these pillars
of inspiration, whose light has made this creation possible.

CONTENTS

ACKNOWLEDGMENTS

With immense gratitude, I extend my heartfelt appreciation to Ms. Jayshree R. of Coimbatore, whose invaluable teachings during my initial learning program at Tata Consultancy Services laid the foundation for my understanding of computing. Her clarity of thought, patience, and passion for imparting knowledge kindled my curiosity and gave me the confidence to explore the vast realm of technology.

I am deeply indebted to my parents, whose unwavering love, encouragement, and sacrifices have been the cornerstone of my journey. Their constant support and belief in my potential have given me the strength to overcome challenges and pursue my passions.

This book is a testament to the lessons, values, and inspiration I have been fortunate to receive from all of them, and I express my deepest gratitude for their invaluable contributions to my life.

1 INTRODUCTION TO COMPUTING AND PROGRAMMING BASICS

1.1 Understanding Computers and Software

In today's technology-driven world, computers serve as the backbone of almost every industry. From communication and transportation to healthcare and entertainment, their omnipresence is undeniable. But what exactly is a computer? At its core, a computer is a device capable of processing information to perform tasks, solve problems, and facilitate communication. Understanding how computers work and the programming that powers them is the first step toward leveraging their full potential.

1.2 Basics of Computer Architecture

A computer system is like a symphony orchestra, where each component plays its part to produce harmonious functionality. The fundamental components of a computer include the CPU (Central Processing Unit), memory, and storage.

1.2.1 The CPU: The Brain of the Computer

The Central Processing Unit (CPU) is often referred to as the "brain" of the computer. It is responsible for executing instructions and performing calculations. Modern CPUs are designed with multiple cores, enabling them to handle several tasks simultaneously, a feature critical in today's multitasking environments.

Each CPU consists of two main parts:

The Arithmetic Logic Unit (ALU): This handles arithmetic and logical operations.
The Control Unit (CU): This directs data flow between the CPU and other computer components.
The performance of a CPU depends on several factors, including clock speed (measured in GHz), the number of cores, and the size of the cache memory.

1.2.2 Memory: The Short-Term Workspace

Computers utilize two types of memory:
RAM (Random Access Memory): Temporary storage that holds data and instructions currently being processed.
ROM (Read-Only Memory): Non-volatile storage that contains essential instructions for booting up the computer.
The efficiency of memory significantly affects the speed and performance of a computer.

1.2.3 Storage: Long-Term Data Repository

Unlike memory, storage is used to retain data even when the computer is turned off. There are two primary types:

Hard Disk Drives (HDDs): Cost-effective and capable of storing large amounts of data.
Solid State Drives (SSDs): Faster and more durable, though generally more expensive.
Modern systems often use a combination of both, with SSDs for the operating system and frequently used programs, and

HDDs for bulk storage.

1.3 Operating Systems: Windows, Linux, and macOS

The Operating System (OS) acts as an intermediary between hardware and software, managing resources and providing a user-friendly interface. Different operating systems are tailored to varying needs, each with its strengths and weaknesses.

1.3.1 Windows

Microsoft Windows is one of the most widely used operating systems, known for its versatility and compatibility with a wide range of hardware and software. It features a graphical user interface (GUI) and tools that cater to both novice users and professionals. Popular versions include Windows 10 and Windows 11.

Advantages:
- ✓ Broad software support.
- ✓ User-friendly interface.
- ✓ Regular updates and security patches.

Challenges:
- ✗ Susceptible to malware and viruses.
- ✗ Licensing costs.

1.3.2 Linux

Linux is an open-source operating system known for its flexibility and security. It is highly favored by developers, engineers, and enthusiasts. Common distributions (distros) include Ubuntu, Fedora, and CentOS.

Advantages:
- ✓ Open-source and free to use.
- ✓ Highly customizable.
- ✓ Superior security features.

Challenges:
- ✗ Steeper learning curve for beginners.

✖ Limited support for proprietary software.

1.3.3 macOS

Developed by Apple, macOS is renowned for its sleek design and seamless integration with Apple's ecosystem. It is widely used by professionals in creative industries.

Advantages:
- ✓ Optimized performance on Apple hardware.
- ✓ Strong focus on aesthetics and usability.
- ✓ Enhanced security features.

Challenges:
- ✖ Higher hardware costs.
- ✖ Limited compatibility with non-Apple devices.

1.4 Introduction to Software Tools Used in Programming

Programming is the process of creating a set of instructions for a computer to execute tasks. Various tools are available to simplify this process, each catering to specific needs and skill levels.

1.4.1 Integrated Development Environments (IDEs)

An Integrated Development Environment (IDE) is a software application that combines essential programming tools into one interface. Popular IDEs include:

Visual Studio Code: Lightweight, highly extensible, and supports multiple programming languages.
Eclipse: A powerful IDE commonly used for Java development.
PyCharm: Tailored for Python, with features that streamline coding and debugging.

1.4.2 Text Editors

For those who prefer minimalism, text editors are a great choice. Popular options include:

Notepad++: Lightweight and beginner-friendly.
Sublime Text: Known for its speed and customizable interface.
Vim: Favored by advanced users for its efficiency and keyboard-centric navigation.

1.4.3 Version Control Systems
Collaborative projects often require version control to track changes and manage code repositories. Common tools include:

Git: A distributed version control system used to manage code efficiently.
GitHub: A cloud-based platform for hosting Git repositories and collaborating on projects.

1.4.4 Debugging Tools
Debugging is an essential part of programming, and various tools can assist in identifying and fixing errors:

GDB: The GNU Debugger, primarily used for C and C++ programs.
Chrome DevTools: A web-based debugging tool for JavaScript and web applications.
Postman: Ideal for testing APIs and debugging network requests.

1.4.5 Command Line Tools
While graphical interfaces dominate, the command line remains a powerful tool for programmers. Familiarity with basic commands can significantly enhance productivity. For instance:
Bash: A popular shell used in Linux environments.
PowerShell: A task automation framework for Windows.

1.5 Conclusion
Understanding the basics of computing and programming is a pivotal first step in the journey toward mastering technology. By grasping the fundamentals of computer architecture,

operating systems, and programming tools, learners can build a solid foundation for more advanced topics.

As you proceed through this book, you will delve deeper into the fascinating world of programming, exploring concepts that empower you to harness the full potential of computers and software. Let this chapter serve as your launchpad into the ever-evolving domain of technology.

Questions with Solutions

1. Understanding Computers and Software

Q1: Define a computer. What are its primary functions?
Solution:
A computer is an electronic device capable of processing data to perform specific tasks. Its primary functions are:
Input: Receiving data through input devices like keyboards or sensors.
Processing: Using the CPU to perform calculations and execute instructions.
Storage: Saving data for temporary or long-term use in memory or storage devices.
Output: Displaying results through output devices like monitors or printers.

2. Basics of Computer Architecture

Q2: Explain the role of the CPU in a computer. What are its main components?
Solution:
The CPU, or Central Processing Unit, is the brain of the computer. It executes instructions and performs calculations. Its main components are:
The Arithmetic Logic Unit (ALU), which handles arithmetic and logical operations.
The Control Unit (CU), which manages the flow of data between the CPU and other components.

Q3: Differentiate between RAM and ROM.
Solution:
RAM (Random Access Memory) is volatile memory that temporarily stores data and instructions the computer is currently using. It is fast but loses data when the computer is powered off.

ROM (Read-Only Memory) is non-volatile memory that permanently stores essential instructions, such as those needed for booting the computer. It retains data even when the computer is turned off.

Q4: What are the advantages of SSDs over HDDs?
Solution:
SSDs, or Solid State Drives, offer several advantages over HDDs (Hard Disk Drives), including:
Faster data access and shorter boot times.
Greater durability since SSDs have no moving parts.
Lower energy consumption, making them more power-efficient.

3. Operating Systems

Q5: List two advantages and two challenges of using Linux as an operating system.
Solution:
Advantages of Linux include its open-source nature, which makes it free and customizable, and its strong security features. Challenges include its steeper learning curve for beginners and limited support for proprietary software.

Q6: Match the following operating systems with their characteristics:
Windows: Known for broad compatibility with software and hardware.
Linux: Recognized for being open-source and highly secure.
macOS: Designed for seamless integration with Apple hardware and a strong focus on aesthetics.
Solution:
Windows is compatible with a wide range of software and hardware.
Linux is open-source and secure.
macOS is optimized for Apple hardware and emphasizes design.

BASIC ARTIFICIAL INTELLIGENCE SKILLS

4. Software Tools Used in Programming

Q7: What is an IDE, and how does it differ from a text editor?
Solution:
An IDE (Integrated Development Environment) is a software application that provides a complete suite of tools for programming, including a code editor, debugger, and compiler. In contrast, a text editor is a lightweight tool used for writing plain text or code without advanced features like debugging or automation.

Q8: Identify three popular tools for version control and explain their purpose.
Solution:
Git: A distributed version control system used for tracking code changes.
GitHub: A platform for hosting and sharing Git repositories, enabling collaboration.
Bitbucket: Another platform for managing Git repositories, often used in team projects.

Q9: What makes Visual Studio Code popular among developers?
Solution:
Visual Studio Code is lightweight, supports multiple programming languages, is highly extensible, and integrates well with version control systems like Git.

Q10: Explain the purpose of debugging tools. Name two commonly used debugging tools.
Solution:
Debugging tools are used to identify and fix errors in code. Examples include:
GDB (GNU Debugger) for debugging C and C++ programs. Chrome DevTools for debugging JavaScript and web applications.

5. Miscellaneous

Q11: Why is the command line still important for programmers?

Solution:

The command line provides direct access to the operating system, allowing faster execution of tasks, automation, and efficient debugging, which can be more powerful than graphical interfaces.

Q12: Fill in the blanks:

The _____ is the brain of the computer.

Ubuntu is a popular distribution of _____.

The two types of computer storage are _____ and _____.

Solution:

CPU.

Linux.

HDD and SSD.

2 PROGRAMMING FUNDAMENTALS

Programming is the art of instructing a computer to perform specific tasks. It involves creating a sequence of instructions that the computer executes to produce desired outputs. This chapter delves into the foundational aspects of programming, focusing on syntax, variables, data types, control structures, and writing basic programs in C and Java.

2.1 Basics of Coding: Syntax, Variables, and Data Types

2.1.1 Syntax
In programming, syntax refers to the set of rules that define the structure of valid statements in a programming language. Just as grammar governs the correctness of sentences in a natural language, syntax ensures that the instructions provided to a computer are interpretable.

Every programming language has its unique syntax. For instance:
In C, statements end with a semicolon (;).
In Java, code is organized into classes and methods.

A syntactically incorrect program will fail to compile, making syntax one of the most critical elements of coding.

2.1.2 Variables
A variable is a named storage location in memory, used to store data that can be modified during program execution. Variables are declared with specific data types, which define the kind of data they can hold.

Example in C:

int age = 25; // Declares an integer variable named 'age' and initializes it with 25.

Example in Java:

String name = "Alice"; // Declares a string variable named 'name' and initializes it with "Alice".

2.1.3 Data Types
Data types define the type of data a variable can hold. Common data types include:

Integer (int): For whole numbers.
Float (float): For decimal numbers.
Character (char): For single characters.
String: For text (Java provides a built-in String type, while C uses character arrays).
Boolean: For true/false values.

2.2 Control Structures: Loops and Conditional Statements
Control structures are the building blocks of logic in programming. They allow the program to make decisions and repeat tasks based on conditions.

2.2.1 Conditional Statements
Conditional statements enable a program to execute a specific

block of code based on whether a condition is true or false.

1. If-Else Statement
In C:

```c
if (age >= 18) {
   printf("You are eligible to vote.\n");
} else {
   printf("You are not eligible to vote.\n");
}
```

In Java:

```java
if (age >= 18) {
   System.out.println("You are eligible to vote.");
} else {
   System.out.println("You are not eligible to vote.");
}
```

2. Switch Statement
The switch statement is useful when multiple conditions need to be checked.

C Example:

```c
switch (day) {
   case 1: printf("Monday\n"); break;
   case 2: printf("Tuesday\n"); break;
   default: printf("Invalid day\n");
}
```

Java Example:

```java
switch (day) {
   case 1: System.out.println("Monday"); break;
   case 2: System.out.println("Tuesday"); break;
   default: System.out.println("Invalid day");
}
```

2.2.2 Loops

Loops are used to execute a block of code repeatedly as long as a condition is met.

1. For Loop
In C:

```
for (int i = 0; i < 5; i++) {
    printf("Iteration %d\n", i);
}
```

In Java:

```
for (int i = 0; i < 5; i++) {
    System.out.println("Iteration " + i);
}
```

2. While Loop
In C:

```
int i = 0;
while (i < 5) {
    printf("Iteration %d\n", i);
    i++;
}
```

In Java:

```
int i = 0;
while (i < 5) {
    System.out.println("Iteration " + i);
    i++;
}
```

3. Do-While Loop
In C:

```
int i = 0;
```

```
do {
  printf("Iteration %d\n", i);
  i++;
} while (i < 5);
```

In Java:

```
int i = 0;
do {
  System.out.println("Iteration " + i);
  i++;
} while (i < 5);
```

2.3 Writing Simple Programs in C and Java
2.3.1 A Simple C Program: Sum of Two Numbers

```
#include <stdio.h>

int main() {
  int num1, num2, sum;
  printf("Enter two numbers: ");
  scanf("%d %d", &num1, &num2);
  sum = num1 + num2;
  printf("The sum is: %d\n", sum);
  return 0;
}
```

2.3.2 A Simple Java Program: Sum of Two Numbers

```
import java.util.Scanner;

public class SumCalculator {
  public static void main(String[] args) {
    Scanner scanner = new Scanner(System.in);
    System.out.print("Enter first number: ");
    int num1 = scanner.nextInt();
    System.out.print("Enter second number: ");
    int num2 = scanner.nextInt();
```

```
    int sum = num1 + num2;
    System.out.println("The sum is: " + sum);
  }
}
```

2.3.3 A Simple C Program: Checking Even or Odd

```c
#include <stdio.h>

int main() {
  int num;
  printf("Enter a number: ");
  scanf("%d", &num);
  if (num % 2 == 0) {
    printf("The number is even.\n");
  } else {
    printf("The number is odd.\n");
  }
  return 0;
}
```

2.3.4 A Simple Java Program: Checking Even or Odd

```java
import java.util.Scanner;

public class EvenOddChecker {
  public static void main(String[] args) {
    Scanner scanner = new Scanner(System.in);
    System.out.print("Enter a number: ");
    int num = scanner.nextInt();
    if (num % 2 == 0) {
      System.out.println("The number is even.");
    } else {
      System.out.println("The number is odd.");
    }
  }
}
```

2.4 Conclusion

This chapter introduced the basics of programming, including syntax, variables, data types, and control structures, followed by practical examples in C and Java. These fundamental concepts form the building blocks of all programming endeavors.

By mastering these basics, you are equipped to tackle more complex problems, enabling you to create efficient and functional programs. In subsequent chapters, we will explore advanced concepts such as functions, object-oriented programming, and data structures, paving the way for a deeper understanding of software development.

BASIC ARTIFICIAL INTELLIGENCE SKILLS

Questions with Solutions

1. Basics of Coding: Syntax, Variables, and Data Types
Q1: What is the importance of syntax in programming?
Solution: Syntax is crucial in programming because it defines the rules for writing valid code that a compiler or interpreter can understand. Errors in syntax prevent the program from compiling or running. For example, missing a semicolon in C or improperly closed braces in Java will lead to syntax errors.

Q2: Write the correct syntax to declare a variable age as an integer in C and Java.
Solution:
In C: **int age;**

In Java: **int age;**

Q3: What are the main data types in programming? Provide examples of each.
Solution:
The main data types are:
Integer (int): Stores whole numbers.
Example: int num = 10;.
Float (float): Stores decimal numbers.
Example: float num = 10.5;.
Character (char): Stores single characters.
Example: char letter = 'A';.
String: Stores text.
Example: String name = "Alice"; (Java).
Boolean: Stores true or false values.
Example: boolean isTrue = true;.
2. Control Structures: Loops and Conditional Statements

Q4: Explain the difference between if-else and switch statements with an example for each in C.
Solution: If-Else: Used for decision-making when conditions involve comparisons or logical operators. Example:

```
if (age >= 18) {
   printf("You are eligible to vote.\n");
} else {
   printf("You are not eligible to vote.\n");
}
```

Switch: Used for multiple predefined conditions with specific values. Example:

```
switch (day) {
   case 1: printf("Monday\n"); break;
   case 2: printf("Tuesday\n"); break;
   default: printf("Invalid day\n");
}
```

Q5: What is the purpose of loops in programming? Name three types of loops and explain one with an example in Java.
Solution:
Loops allow repetitive execution of a block of code as long as a condition is met.
Types of loops:

- For Loop
- While Loop
- Do-While Loop

Example of a for loop in Java:

```
for (int i = 0; i < 5; i++) {
   System.out.println("Iteration " + i);
}
```

This loop runs 5 times, incrementing i from 0 to 4.

Q6: Write a program in C to print numbers from 1 to 10 using a while loop.
Solution:

```
#include <stdio.h>

int main() {
```

```c
  int i = 1;
  while (i <= 10) {
    printf("%d\n", i);
    i++;
  }
  return 0;
}
```

3. Writing Simple Programs in C and Java

Q7: Write a program in Java to check if a number is even or odd.
Solution:

```java
import java.util.Scanner;

public class EvenOddChecker {
  public static void main(String[] args) {
    Scanner scanner = new Scanner(System.in);
    System.out.print("Enter a number: ");
    int num = scanner.nextInt();
    if (num % 2 == 0) {
      System.out.println("The number is even.");
    } else {
      System.out.println("The number is odd.");
    }
  }
}
```

Q8: Create a program in C to calculate the sum of two numbers entered by the user.
Solution:

```c
#include <stdio.h>

int main() {
  int num1, num2, sum;
  printf("Enter two numbers: ");
```

```
scanf("%d %d", &num1, &num2);
sum = num1 + num2;
printf("The sum is: %d\n", sum);
return 0;
}
```

Q9: Explain the purpose of the do-while loop with an example in Java.
Solution: The do-while loop ensures that the block of code runs at least once, even if the condition is false.

Example in Java:

```
int i = 0;
do {
    System.out.println("Iteration " + i);
    i++;
} while (i < 5);
```

Here, the code inside the loop runs once before checking if i < 5.

Q10: Write a C program to find the factorial of a given number using a for loop.
Solution:

```
#include <stdio.h>

int main() {
    int num, factorial = 1;
    printf("Enter a number: ");
    scanf("%d", &num);
    for (int i = 1; i <= num; i++) {
        factorial *= i;
    }
    printf("The factorial of %d is %d\n", num, factorial);
    return 0;
}
```

3 DEBUGGING AND CODE OPTIMIZATION

Debugging and code optimization are fundamental skills for any programmer, shaping the quality, reliability, and efficiency of the software they develop. While debugging focuses on identifying and fixing errors, optimization aims to improve the performance and scalability of the code. This chapter explores these topics in depth, providing insights into common errors, effective debugging techniques, best practices for writing efficient code, and hands-on exercises to hone these skills.

3.1 Understanding Common Errors and Debugging Techniques

Errors, also known as bugs, are inevitable in programming. They occur for various reasons, such as logical flaws, incorrect syntax, or unforeseen edge cases. Recognizing and addressing these errors is essential to ensure program correctness.

3.1.1 Types of Errors

Syntax Errors:

Syntax errors arise when the code violates the rules of the programming language. These are typically detected by the

compiler or interpreter.
Example in C:

printf("Hello World") // Missing semicolon causes a syntax error.
Solution: Add a semicolon at the end:

printf("Hello World");

Logical Errors:
These errors occur when the program runs without crashing but produces incorrect results. Logical errors are challenging to detect as they don't halt execution.
Example in Java:

int sum = a - b; // Incorrect operator used for addition.
Solution: Use the correct operator:

int sum = a + b;

Runtime Errors:
These occur during program execution, such as dividing by zero or accessing an invalid array index.
Example in C:

int x = 10 / 0; // Division by zero causes a runtime error.
Solution: Ensure the denominator is not zero:

```
if (denominator != 0) {
    int result = numerator / denominator;
}
```

3.1.2 Debugging Techniques
Debugging involves systematically identifying and resolving errors in code. Effective debugging techniques include:

Using Debuggers:
Tools like GDB (GNU Debugger) for C and Eclipse

Debugger for Java allow step-by-step code execution to identify the source of errors.

Print Statements:
Adding print statements to display variable values and program flow helps locate logical errors.
Example in C:

printf("Value of x: %d\n", x);
Logging:
Incorporating logs provides a detailed record of program execution, which is particularly useful for debugging complex systems.

Breakpoints:
Setting breakpoints pauses program execution at specific lines, allowing inspection of variable states.

Code Review:
Peer reviews often reveal overlooked errors and improve code quality.

3.2 Writing Efficient Code: Best Practices
Writing efficient code involves creating programs that are not only correct but also optimized for speed, memory usage, and scalability.

3.2.1 Principles of Efficient Coding

Clarity Over Cleverness:
Write clear and readable code, even if it means sacrificing minor optimizations. Code clarity aids debugging and future maintenance.

Avoid Redundancy:
Reuse code through functions or methods instead of duplicating it.

Use Data Structures Wisely:
Select the appropriate data structure for the task. For example, use a hash table for fast lookups and a linked list for frequent insertions.

Optimize Loops:
Reduce the number of iterations or eliminate unnecessary computations inside loops.
Example:

```
for (int i = 0; i < n; i++) {
   for (int j = 0; j < n; j++) {
      // Avoid redundant calculations inside the loop.
   }
}
```

Minimize Memory Usage:
Free unused memory and avoid excessive allocations.

3.2.2 Tools for Code Optimization

Profiling Tools:
Identify bottlenecks in code using tools like gprof for C or VisualVM for Java.

Compiler Optimization:
Enable optimization flags during compilation, such as -O2 or -O3 in GCC for better performance.

Static Code Analysis:
Tools like SonarQube help detect inefficient code patterns and suggest improvements.

3.3 Hands-On Activity: Fixing and Optimizing Basic Programs
Let's apply debugging and optimization techniques to improve two example programs.

3.3.1 Example 1: Fixing a Program to Calculate Factorial (C)
Original Code:

```c
#include <stdio.h>
int main() {
   int num = 5, fact = 1;
   for (int i = 0; i <= num; i++) {  // Logical error: i should start from 1.
      fact = fact * i;
   }
   printf("Factorial: %d\n", fact);
   return 0;
}
```

Issues:
The loop starts from 0, causing multiplication by 0.
No input handling for user-specified numbers.
Optimized Code:

```c
#include <stdio.h>
int main() {
   int num, fact = 1;
   printf("Enter a number: ");
   scanf("%d", &num);
   for (int i = 1; i <= num; i++) {
      fact *= i;   // Optimized by using shorthand operator.
   }
   printf("Factorial: %d\n", fact);
   return 0;
}
```

3.3.2 Example 2: Optimizing a Search Program (Java)
Original Code:

```java
public class LinearSearch {
   public static void main(String[] args) {
```

```java
        int[] arr = {1, 2, 3, 4, 5};
        int target = 3;
        for (int i = 0; i < arr.length; i++) {
            if (arr[i] == target) {
                System.out.println("Found at index " + i);
            }
        }
    }
}
```
Issues:

The loop continues even after finding the target.

No user input for the array or target value.

Optimized Code:

```java
import java.util.Scanner;

public class LinearSearch {
    public static void main(String[] args) {
        Scanner scanner = new Scanner(System.in);
        System.out.print("Enter the size of the array: ");
        int n = scanner.nextInt();
        int[] arr = new int[n];
        System.out.println("Enter the array elements:");
        for (int i = 0; i < n; i++) {
            arr[i] = scanner.nextInt();
        }
        System.out.print("Enter the target value: ");
        int target = scanner.nextInt();

        boolean found = false;
        for (int i = 0; i < arr.length; i++) {
            if (arr[i] == target) {
                System.out.println("Found at index " + i);
                found = true;
                break;  // Optimization: Exit loop after finding target.
            }
        }
```

```
  if (!found) {
    System.out.println("Target not found.");
  }
 }
}
```

3.4 Conclusion

Debugging and code optimization are iterative processes essential to developing reliable and efficient software. By understanding common errors and employing effective debugging techniques, programmers can ensure their code runs as intended. Furthermore, adopting best practices for code efficiency not only enhances performance but also ensures scalability and maintainability.

Through hands-on activities, this chapter demonstrated how to identify, fix, and optimize programs, setting the stage for advanced software development in future chapters.

BASIC ARTIFICIAL INTELLIGENCE SKILLS

Questions with Solutions

1. Understanding Common Errors and Debugging Techniques

Q1: Define debugging. Why is it important in programming?
Solution: Debugging is the process of identifying, analyzing, and resolving errors (bugs) in a program. It is important because:
It ensures the program functions as intended.
It improves program reliability and user experience.
It helps maintain code quality and prevents future issues.

Q2: What are the three common types of errors in programming? Provide an example for each.
Solution:
Syntax Errors: Violations of language rules detected by the compiler.
Example: Missing a semicolon in C:

printf("Hello World") // Syntax error.
Logical Errors: Errors in program logic producing incorrect results.
Example: Using subtraction instead of addition:

int sum = a - b; // Logical error.

Runtime Errors: Errors that occur during program execution, such as division by zero.
Example:

int x = 10 / 0; // Runtime error.

Q3: Explain the purpose of breakpoints in debugging.
Solution:Breakpoints pause the execution of a program at specific lines of code, allowing the programmer to inspect variable values, program flow, and the state of the system. This helps identify the source of errors more effectively.

Q4: What is the difference between debugging using print statements and logging?
Solution: Print Statements: Temporarily added to display variable values or program flow during debugging. They are usually removed after debugging.
Logging: Provides a persistent record of program execution, including timestamps and error details, and is often retained in production systems.

2. Writing Efficient Code: Best Practices

Q5: What are the principles of efficient coding?
Solution: Write clear and readable code.
Avoid redundant code by reusing functions.
Use appropriate data structures for the task.
Optimize loops to minimize unnecessary computations.
Free unused memory to reduce resource consumption.

Q6: Why is selecting the correct data structure important? Provide an example.
Solution: Choosing the right data structure ensures better performance and resource efficiency.
Example:
Using a hash table for fast lookups instead of a linked list, which requires traversing elements sequentially.

Q7: Identify and explain two tools used for code optimization.
Solution:

Profiling Tools: Analyze program execution to identify bottlenecks. Examples: gprof (C), VisualVM (Java).
Static Code Analysis Tools: Detect inefficient code patterns and suggest improvements. Examples: SonarQube, Pylint.

3. Hands-On Activity: Fixing and Optimizing Basic Programs

Q8: Fix the following C program to calculate the factorial of a number. Identify and correct the error.

Original Code:

```
#include <stdio.h>

int main() {
    int num = 5, fact = 1;
    for (int i = 0; i <= num; i++) {  // Error: Loop starts
at 0.
        fact = fact * i;
    }
    printf("Factorial: %d\n", fact);
    return 0;
}
```

Solution:
The loop should start from 1, as multiplying by 0 results in 0.
Corrected Code:

```
#include <stdio.h>

int main() {
    int num = 5, fact = 1;
    for (int i = 1; i <= num; i++) {
        fact *= i;
    }
    printf("Factorial: %d\n", fact);
    return 0;
}
```

Q9: Optimize the following Java program for linear search.
Original Code:

```
public class LinearSearch {
    public static void main(String[] args) {
        int[] arr = {1, 2, 3, 4, 5};
        int target = 3;
        for (int i = 0; i < arr.length; i++) {
            if (arr[i] == target) {
```

```
        System.out.println("Found at index " + i);
      }
    }
  }
}
```

Solution:
The program unnecessarily continues searching after finding the target. Add a break statement to stop the loop once the target is found.
Optimized Code:

```
public class LinearSearch {
  public static void main(String[] args) {
    int[] arr = {1, 2, 3, 4, 5};
    int target = 3;
    for (int i = 0; i < arr.length; i++) {
      if (arr[i] == target) {
        System.out.println("Found at index " + i);
        break;  // Stop searching once target is found.
      }
    }
  }
}
```

Q10: Write a program in C to detect and handle division by zero.
Solution:

```
#include <stdio.h>

int main() {
  int numerator, denominator;
  printf("Enter numerator: ");
  scanf("%d", &numerator);
  printf("Enter denominator: ");
  scanf("%d", &denominator);
```

```
if (denominator != 0) {
    printf("Result: %d\n", numerator / denominator);
} else {
    printf("Error: Division by zero is not allowed.\n");
}
return 0;
}
```

Q11: Explain how a profiling tool can help optimize a program.
Solution:
Profiling tools analyze a program's runtime behavior to identify bottlenecks, such as slow functions or inefficient loops. For instance, gprof for C can highlight functions consuming the most CPU time, allowing developers to focus their optimization efforts on those areas.

Q12: What is the benefit of using compiler optimization flags, such as -O2 or -O3 in GCC?
Solution:
Compiler optimization flags improve the performance of the code by:

Reducing execution time.
Optimizing memory usage.
Eliminating redundant calculations.
For example, -O3 enables high-level optimizations, including function inlining and loop unrolling.

4 FOUNDATIONS OF MATHEMATICS FOR AI

Mathematics is the backbone of Artificial Intelligence (AI). Among the various mathematical disciplines, Linear Algebra plays a fundamental role in AI, machine learning, and deep learning. AI systems rely on matrices, vectors, and linear transformations for data representation, manipulation, and processing. In this chapter, we will explore the basics of Linear Algebra, focusing on vectors, matrices, their operations, and the role of matrix multiplication in AI.

4.1 Understanding Vectors

Vectors are one of the most fundamental concepts in Linear Algebra. A vector is an ordered collection of numbers, often used to represent points, directions, or features in AI systems.

4.1.1 Definition of a Vector

A vector is an element of a vector space, represented as a column or row of numbers:

Column vector (3-dimensional):

$$v = \begin{bmatrix} v_1 \\ v_2 \\ v_3 \end{bmatrix}$$

Row vector (3-dimensional):

$$v = \begin{bmatrix} v_1 & v_2 & v_3 \end{bmatrix}$$

4.2 Vector Operations

4.2.1 Addition and Subtraction

Vectors of the same dimension can be added or subtracted component-wise:

$$a + b = \begin{bmatrix} a_1 + b_1 \\ a_2 + b_2 \\ a_3 + b_3 \end{bmatrix}$$

4.2.2 Scalar Multiplication

A vector can be multiplied by a scalar (constant) to scale its magnitude:

$$c.v = \begin{bmatrix} c.v_1 \\ c.v_2 \\ c.v_3 \end{bmatrix}$$

4.2.3 Dot Product (Inner Product)

The dot product of two vectors results in a scalar and is computed as:

$$a.b = a_1 b_1 + a_2 b_2 + a_3 b_3$$

The dot product is useful in AI for calculating similarities between data points.

4.2.4 Cross Product

For 3D vectors, the cross-product results in another vector:

$$a \times b = \begin{bmatrix} a_2 b_3 - a_3 b_2 \\ a_3 b_1 - a_1 b_3 \\ a_1 b_2 - a_2 b_1 \end{bmatrix}$$

The cross product is widely used in robotics and physics simulations.

4.3 Matrices and Their Operations

A matrix is a rectangular array of numbers arranged in rows and columns. Matrices are heavily used in AI for transformations, data representation, and neural networks.

4.3.1 Definition of a Matrix

A matrix with dimensions (rows, columns) is represented as:

$$A = \begin{bmatrix} a_{11} & .. & a_{1n} \\ .. & .. & .. \\ a_{m1} & .. & a_{mn} \end{bmatrix}$$

4.4 Matrix Operations

4.4.1 Addition and Subtraction

Two matrices of the same dimensions can be added or subtracted component-wise:

$$A + B = \begin{bmatrix} a_{11} + b_{11} & a_{12} + b_{12} \\ a_{21} + b_{21} & a_{22} + b_{22} \end{bmatrix}$$

4.4.2 Scalar Multiplication

Each element of a matrix can be multiplied by a scalar:

$$cA = \begin{bmatrix} ca_{11} & ca_{12} \\ ca_{21} & ca_{22} \end{bmatrix}$$

4.4.3 Matrix Transposition

Swapping rows with columns results in the transpose of a matrix:

$$A^T = \begin{bmatrix} a_{11} & a_{21} \\ a_{12} & a_{22} \end{bmatrix}$$

4.5 Matrix Multiplication and Its Role in AI

Matrix multiplication is essential in AI, as it is used in transformations, neural networks, and optimization problems.

4.5.1 Matrix Multiplication Rules

Matrix multiplication follows specific rules:

If A is an $m \times n$ matrix and B is an $n \times p$ matrix, their product AB is an $m \times p$ matrix.

The elements of the result matrix are computed as:

$$C_{ij} = \sum_{k=1}^{n} A_{ik} B_{kj}$$

Example:

$$A = \begin{bmatrix} 1 & 2 \\ 3 & 4 \end{bmatrix}, B = \begin{bmatrix} 5 & 6 \\ 7 & 8 \end{bmatrix}$$

$$AB = \begin{bmatrix} \{(1 \times 5) + (2 \times 7)\} & \{(1 \times 6) + (2 \times 8)\} \\ \{(3 \times 5) + (4 \times 7)\} & \{(3 \times 6) + (4 \times 8)\} \end{bmatrix}$$
$$= \begin{bmatrix} 19 & 22 \\ 43 & 50 \end{bmatrix}$$

4.6 Applications in AI

4.6.1 Neural Networks

Neural networks heavily rely on matrix multiplication to process large datasets efficiently. Input layers, hidden layers, and output layers are represented using matrices.

4.6.2 Image Processing

Images are represented as matrices, where each pixel corresponds to an element in the matrix. Matrix multiplication is used in image filters, where convolution operations apply different filters to an image for edge detection, sharpening, and blurring. Transformations such as rotation, scaling, and translation are performed using transformation matrices. Feature extraction techniques, such as Principal Component Analysis (PCA), leverage matrix operations to reduce dimensionality and extract significant features from image datasets.

4.6.3 Recommendation Systems

Matrix factorization techniques are used to suggest relevant items based on user preferences.

4.7 Conclusion

In this chapter, we covered fundamental Linear Algebra concepts crucial for AI. Understanding vectors, matrices, and their operations forms the foundation for advanced AI topics like deep learning, image processing, and optimization. Mastering these basics allows AI practitioners to build robust models and efficiently manipulate high-dimensional data. As we progress, we will explore more mathematical tools essential for AI applications.

This chapter establishes a strong mathematical foundation for AI, equipping readers with essential concepts needed to delve into more complex topics in artificial intelligence and machine learning.

Questions with Solutions

Q1: What is a vector, and how is it represented in Linear Algebra?

Solution: A vector is an ordered collection of numbers that represent a point in space, direction, or set of features. It can be represented as a column vector:

$$v = \begin{bmatrix} v_1 \\ v_2 \\ v_3 \end{bmatrix}$$

or as a row vector:

$$v = \begin{bmatrix} v_1 & v_2 & v_3 \end{bmatrix}$$

Q2: How does matrix multiplication work?

Solution: Matrix multiplication follows the rule that if A is an $m \times n$ matrix and B is an $n \times p$ matrix, their product AB is an $m \times p$ matrix.

The elements of the result matrix are computed as:

$$C_{ij} = \sum_{k=1}^{n} A_{ik} B_{kj}$$

Example:

$$A = \begin{bmatrix} 1 & 2 \\ 3 & 4 \end{bmatrix}, B = \begin{bmatrix} 5 & 6 \\ 7 & 8 \end{bmatrix}$$

$$AB = \begin{bmatrix} \{(1 \times 5) + (2 \times 7)\} & \{(1 \times 6) + (2 \times 8)\} \\ \{(3 \times 5) + (4 \times 7)\} & \{(3 \times 6) + (4 \times 8)\} \end{bmatrix}$$
$$= \begin{bmatrix} 19 & 22 \\ 43 & 50 \end{bmatrix}$$

Q3: What is the significance of the dot product in AI?
Solution: The dot product measures the similarity between two vectors. It is widely used in AI applications like recommendation systems and classification. If the dot product is zero, the vectors are orthogonal, meaning they have no correlation.

Q4: Why is Singular Value Decomposition (SVD) important in AI?
Solution: SVD is used for dimensionality reduction, noise filtering, and feature extraction. It is commonly applied in image compression, text analysis, and recommendation systems.

Q5: Compute the dot product of vectors
$$a = [3,4,5] \text{ and } b = [1,2,3].$$
Solution:
$a \cdot b = (3 \times 1) + (4 \times 2) + (5 \times 3) = 3+8+15 = 26$

Q6: Given the matrices:
$A = \begin{bmatrix} 1 & 2 \\ 3 & 4 \end{bmatrix}, B = \begin{bmatrix} 2 & 0 \\ 1 & 3 \end{bmatrix}$ find AB
Solution:

$$AB = \begin{bmatrix} (1 \times 2 + 2 \times 1) & (1 \times 0 + 2 \times 3) \\ (3 \times 2 + 4 \times 1) & (3 \times 0 + 4 \times 3) \end{bmatrix}$$
$$= \begin{bmatrix} 4 & 6 \\ 10 & 12 \end{bmatrix}$$

5 PROBABILITY AND STATISTICS FOR AI

Probability and statistics are integral components of Artificial Intelligence (AI). These mathematical tools enable machines to make informed decisions, analyze uncertainties, and model real-world phenomena. From predicting customer preferences to optimizing machine learning models, probability and statistics are widely used in AI applications.

This chapter will provide a deep dive into the fundamental concepts of probability and statistics, including mean, median, mode, and variance, followed by an exploration of probability distributions and Bayes' theorem. Additionally, hands-on programming activities will be included to reinforce these concepts through code.

5.1 Basic Statistical Concepts

Statistics is the science of collecting, analyzing, and interpreting data. It provides methods for understanding trends, making predictions, and supporting decision-making in AI systems.

5.2 Measures of Central Tendency

Measures of central tendency describe the central point of a dataset. The three primary measures are:

5.2.1 Mean (Arithmetic Average)

The mean is the sum of all data points divided by the total number of points:

$$Mean = \frac{\sum_{i=1}^{n} x_i}{n}$$

where x_i represents each data point and n is the number of data points.

Example:

Data: 5,10,15,20,25

$$\text{Mean} = \frac{5+10+15+20+25}{5} = 15$$

5.2.2 Median

The median is the middle value of an ordered dataset. If the dataset has an odd number of elements, the median is the middle element. If even, the median is the average of the two middle elements.

Example:

Data: 5,10,15,20,25

$$\text{Median} = \frac{5+10+15+20+25}{5} = 15 \text{(since it is the middle element)}$$

Data: 5,10,15,20

$$\text{Median} = \frac{10+15}{2} = 12.5$$

5.2.3 Mode

The mode is the most frequently occurring value in a dataset. A dataset can have no mode, one mode (unimodal), or multiple modes (multimodal).

Example:

Data: 5,10,10,15,20,20,20,25

Mode = 20 (since it appears most frequently)

5.3 Measures of Dispersion

Measures of dispersion describe the spread or variability of data points.

5.3.1 Variance

Variance measures the average squared deviation from the mean and is given by:

$$\sigma^2 = \frac{\sum_{i=1}^{n}(x_i - \mu)^2}{n}$$

where μ is the mean.

Example:

Data: 5,10,15

Mean = 10

$$\text{Variance} = \frac{(5-10)^2 + (10-10)^2 + (15-10)^2}{3} = 16.67$$

5.3.2 Standard Deviation

The standard deviation (σ) is the square root of variance and represents the spread of data around the mean.

5.4 Probability Distributions

5.4.1 Probability Basics

Probability is the likelihood of an event occurring and is calculated as:

$$P(A) = \frac{Number\ of\ favourable\ outcomes}{Total\ number\ of\ outcomes}$$

5.5 Common Probability Distributions

5.5.1 Uniform Distribution

In a uniform distribution, all outcomes have equal probability.

$$P(x) = \frac{1}{b-a}, a \leq x \leq b$$

5.5.2 Normal Distribution

A normal distribution is a bell-shaped curve characterized by mean μ and standard deviation σ:

$$P(x) = \frac{1}{\sigma\sqrt{2\pi}} e^{-\frac{(x-\mu)^2}{2\sigma^2}}$$

It is widely used in AI for modeling uncertainties.

5.5.3 Bernoulli and Binomial Distributions

The Bernoulli distribution represents a single trial with two possible outcomes (success or failure).

The binomial distribution extends this to multiple trials:

$$P(X = k) = \binom{n}{k} p^k (1 - p)^{n-k}$$

where p is the probability of success and n is the number of trials.

5.6 Bayes' Theorem

Bayes' theorem provides a way to update probabilities based on new evidence:

$$P(A|B) = \frac{P(B|A)P(A)}{P(B)}$$

This theorem is crucial in AI applications such as spam filtering, medical diagnosis, and machine learning algorithms.

Example:

Suppose a test for a disease has a 98% accuracy, and the disease prevalence is 1%. The probability of having the disease given a positive test result is calculated using Bayes' theorem.

5.7 Hands-On Programming Activities

To solidify these concepts, we will implement small programs in Python.

5.7.1 Calculating Mean, Median, and Mode

```
import statistics

data = [5, 10, 15, 20, 25, 10, 20, 20]
print("Mean:", statistics.mean(data))
print("Median:", statistics.median(data))
print("Mode:", statistics.mode(data))
```

5.7.2 Computing Probability

```
import random

def simulate_probability(event_outcome, total_trials=10000):
    success_count = sum(1 for _ in range(total_trials) if
random.randint(1, 6) == event_outcome)
    return success_count / total_trials

print("Probability of rolling a 3 on a die:",
simulate_probability(3))
```

5.7.3 Applying Bayes' Theorem

```
def bayes_theorem(p_a, p_b_given_a, p_b):
    return (p_b_given_a * p_a) / p_b

p_a = 0.01  # Disease prevalence
p_b_given_a = 0.98  # Sensitivity
p_b = (p_b_given_a * p_a) + ((1 - 0.98) * (1 - p_a))

print("P(Disease | Positive Test):", bayes_theorem(p_a,
p_b_given_a, p_b))
```

5.8 Conclusion

Probability and statistics form the backbone of AI, enabling machines to make data-driven decisions. Understanding these concepts is crucial for building robust AI models. This chapter covered fundamental statistical measures, probability distributions, Bayes' theorem, and hands-on coding exercises. Mastery of these topics will empower AI practitioners to develop sophisticated models that handle uncertainty effectively.

BASIC ARTIFICIAL INTELLIGENCE SKILLS

Questions with Solutions

Q1: What is the difference between mean, median, and mode?

Solution:
- Mean is the arithmetic average of a dataset.
- Median is the middle value when data is ordered.
- Mode is the most frequently occurring value in a dataset.

Q2: Explain variance and standard deviation. Why are they important in AI?

Solution:
Variance measures the spread of data points around the mean.

Standard deviation is the square root of variance and represents data dispersion.

In AI, these measures help assess data variability, crucial for decision-making in machine learning models.

Q3: Define probability and give an example of its application in AI.

Solution:
Probability quantifies the likelihood of an event occurring.

Example: AI models use probability to classify emails as spam or not spam.

Q4: What is Bayes' theorem, and how is it applied in AI?

Solution:
Bayes' theorem updates prior probabilities based on new evidence.

Example: It is used in medical diagnosis to update the probability of a disease given a positive test result.

Q5: Find the mean, median, and mode of the dataset: 2, 4, 4, 6, 8, 10, 10, 10, 12.

Solution:
Mean = (2 + 4 + 4 + 6 + 8 + 10 + 10 + 10 + 12) / 9 = 7.33
Median = 8 (middle value)
Mode = 10 (most frequent)

Q6: Calculate the variance and standard deviation of the dataset: 3, 6, 9, 12, 15.

Solution:
Mean = (3+6+9+12+15)/5 = 9
Variance = $[(3-9)^2 + (6-9)^2 + (9-9)^2 + (12-9)^2 + (15-9)^2]$ / 5
Variance = (36 + 9 + 0 + 9 + 36) / 5 = 18
Standard deviation = $\sqrt{18} \approx 4.24$

Q7: A fair six-sided die is rolled. What is the probability of rolling an even number?

Solution:
Even numbers: {2, 4, 6}
P(Even) = 3/6 = 0.5

Q8: A bag contains 3 red balls, 5 blue balls, and 2 green balls. What is the probability of drawing a blue ball?

Solution:
Total balls = 3 + 5 + 2 = 10
P(Blue) = 5/10 = 0.5

Q9: A certain disease affects 2% of a population. A test for the disease is 95% accurate for infected people and 90% accurate for uninfected people. If a person tests positive, what is the probability they have the disease?

Solution:
P(Disease) = 0.02, P(No Disease) = 0.98

P(Positive | Disease) = 0.95
P(Positive | No Disease) = 1 - 0.90 = 0.10
P(Positive) = (0.95 * 0.02) + (0.10 * 0.98) = 0.019 + 0.098
= 0.117
P(Disease | Positive) = (0.95 * 0.02) / 0.117 = 0.162
Final Probability = 16.2%

Q10: Write a Python function to calculate the mean, median, and mode of a list of numbers.

Solution:

```
import statistics

def compute_stats(data):
    return {
        "Mean": statistics.mean(data),
        "Median": statistics.median(data),
        "Mode": statistics.mode(data)
    }

data = [2, 4, 4, 6, 8, 10, 10, 10, 12]
print(compute_stats(data))
```

Q11: Write a Python function to simulate rolling a die 10,000 times and estimate the probability of rolling a 3.

Solution:

```
import random

def simulate_probability(event_outcome, total_trials=10000):
    success_count = sum(1 for _ in range(total_trials) if random.randint(1, 6) == event_outcome)
    return success_count / total_trials
print("Probability of rolling a 3 on a die:", simulate_probability(3))
```

Q12: Write a Python function to compute Bayes' theorem.

Solution:

```
def bayes_theorem(p_a, p_b_given_a, p_b):
    return (p_b_given_a * p_a) / p_b

p_a = 0.02  # Disease prevalence
p_b_given_a = 0.95  # Sensitivity
p_b = (p_b_given_a * p_a) + ((1 - 0.90) * (1 - p_a))

print("P(Disease | Positive Test):", bayes_theorem(p_a,
p_b_given_a, p_b))
```

6 INTRODUCTION TO CALCULUS: DERIVATIVES AND INTEGRALS - CONCEPTS AND APPLICATIONS IN AI

6.1 Introduction

Calculus, the mathematical study of continuous change, plays an indispensable role in various scientific and engineering domains, particularly in artificial intelligence (AI). The two fundamental branches of calculus, differentiation (dealing with rates of change) and integration (concerned with accumulation), serve as the backbone of optimization techniques, machine learning algorithms, and deep learning models. This chapter explores these essential mathematical concepts and their direct applications in AI, with a particular focus on gradient descent and optimization.

6.2 Differentiation: Understanding Derivatives

6.2.1 Definition of a Derivative

The derivative of a function measures how the function's

53

output value changes as its input changes. Mathematically, the derivative of a function $f(x)$ at a point x is defined as:

$$f'(x) = \lim_{h \to 0} \frac{f(x + h) - f(x)}{h}$$

This definition provides the rate at which the function $f(x)$ changes with respect to x.

6.2.2 Rules of Differentiation

Several key differentiation rules simplify the process of finding derivatives:

- Power Rule: $\frac{d}{dx}[x^n] = nx^{n-1}$

- Product Rule: $\frac{d}{dx}[uv] = u'v + uv'$

- Quotient Rule: $\frac{d}{dx}\left[\frac{u}{v}\right] = \frac{u'v - uv'}{v^2}$

- Chain Rule: $\frac{d}{dx}[f(g(x))] = f'(g(x))g'(x)$

6.2.3 Applications of Derivatives in AI

Gradient Calculation for Optimization

In AI and machine learning, derivatives are crucial for optimizing cost functions. The gradient of a function, represented as the vector of partial derivatives, guides the optimization process by indicating the direction of steepest ascent or descent.

Backpropagation in Neural Networks

Backpropagation is an essential algorithm for training neural networks, which utilizes derivatives to adjust weights through gradient descent. The chain rule is applied to compute gradients for deep networks.

Sensitivity Analysis

Derivatives help determine how small changes in input affect the output, aiding in feature selection and model interpretability in machine learning.

6.3 Integration: Understanding Integrals

6.3.1 Definition of an Integral

Integration is the inverse operation of differentiation. It represents the accumulation of a quantity over an interval. The definite integral of a function $f(x)$ from a to b is given by:

$$\int_a^b f(x)\, dx = F(b) - F(a)$$

where $F(x)$ is the antiderivative of $f(x)$, satisfying $F'(x) = f(x)$.

6.3.2 Fundamental Theorems of Calculus

First Fundamental Theorem: If $F(x)$ is an antiderivative of $f(x)$, then:

$$\int_a^b f(x)\, dx = F(b) - F(a)$$

Second Fundamental Theorem: If $f(x)$ is continuous, then its integral function:

$$F(x) = \int_a^x f(t)\, dt$$

is differentiable, and $F'(x) = f(x)$.

6.3.3 Applications of Integrals in AI

Probability Distributions and Expectation

In AI, integrals are extensively used in probability theory to calculate expectations, variances, and probability distributions. For example, the probability density function (PDF) of a continuous random variable is integrated to find cumulative probabilities.

Loss Function Computation

Certain machine learning loss functions involve integrals. For example, in Bayesian inference, integrals are used to compute the posterior probability distribution.

Neural Network Training Regularization

Integrals are used to implement regularization techniques such as L2 regularization, which prevents overfitting by penalizing large model weights.

6.4 Gradient Descent: An Optimization Paradigm

6.4.1 Basics of Gradient Descent

Gradient descent is an iterative optimization algorithm used to minimize a cost function by adjusting parameters in the direction of the steepest descent. The update rule for a parameter θ is:

$$\theta = \theta - \alpha \frac{dJ}{d\theta}$$

where:
- α is the learning rate,
- J is the cost function.

6.4.2 Types of Gradient Descent

Batch Gradient Descent: Computes the gradient using the entire dataset, leading to slow but stable convergence.

Stochastic Gradient Descent (SGD): Updates parameters using a single random sample, leading to faster updates but higher variance.

Mini-batch Gradient Descent: Balances between batch and stochastic methods by computing gradients over small batches.

6.4.3 Applications of Gradient Descent in AI

Training Deep Neural Networks

Gradient descent, combined with backpropagation, is essential for deep learning models to learn patterns in data efficiently.

Convex Optimization in Machine Learning

Many machine learning algorithms, such as Support Vector Machines and Logistic Regression, rely on gradient descent to find optimal decision boundaries.

Natural Language Processing (NLP) Optimization

Gradient-based optimization is used in transformers and recurrent neural networks (RNNs) to fine-tune word embeddings and sequence models.

6.5 Conclusion

Calculus forms the backbone of AI, enabling optimization techniques such as gradient descent, backpropagation, and probabilistic modeling. The concepts of differentiation and integration allow for precise mathematical formulations that guide machine learning algorithms, ensuring efficient training and improved model accuracy. As AI continues to evolve, a strong understanding of these fundamental principles will remain crucial for developing innovative solutions in deep learning, reinforcement learning, and beyond.

BASIC ARTIFICIAL INTELLIGENCE SKILLS

Questions with Solutions

Q1. Explain the significance of differentiation and integration in AI.

Solution:
Differentiation helps in optimization techniques such as gradient descent, backpropagation in neural networks, and sensitivity analysis. Integration is crucial in probability distributions, loss function computations, and regularization techniques.

Q2. Compute the derivative of the function
$$f(x) = 5x^3 - 4x^2 + 7x - 2.$$

Solution:
$$f'(x) = 15x^2 - 8x + 7$$

Q3. A cost function in a neural network is given by $J(\theta)=\theta^2+4\theta+7$. Compute $\frac{dJ}{d\theta}$ and find the update value for $\theta=3$ when $\alpha=0.1$.

Solution:
First, compute the gradient: $\frac{dJ}{d\theta}=2\theta+4$
At $\theta=3$: $\frac{dJ}{d\theta}=2(3)+4=6+4=10$
Using the gradient descent update rule:
$\theta_{new}=\theta-\alpha\frac{dJ}{d\theta}=3-(0.1\times10)=3-1=2$

Q4. Evaluate the integral
$$\int_1^3 (2x^2 - 3x + 4)dx$$

Solution: Finding the antiderivative:
$$F(x)= 2\frac{x^3}{3} - 3\frac{x^2}{2} + 4x$$

59

Evaluating from 1 to 3:

$$F(3) = 2\frac{3^3}{3} - 3\frac{3^2}{2} + 4.3 = 18 - 13.5 + 12 = 16.5$$

$$F(1) = 2\frac{1^3}{3} - 3\frac{1^2}{2} + 4.1 = 0.67 - 1.5 + 4 = 3.17$$

Integral $= 16.5 - 3.33 = 13.33$

7. Suppose a probability density function (PDF) is given by $f(x) = 3x^2$ for $0 \leq x \leq 2$. Find the probability that X lies between 1 and 2

Solution:

$$P(1 \leq X \leq 2) = \int_1^2 3x^2 \, dx = [x^3]_1^2 = [8 - 1] = 7.$$

7 DATA HANDLING AND PREPROCESSING

7.1 Introduction

In the era of big data and artificial intelligence, the ability to handle and preprocess data efficiently is crucial for drawing meaningful insights. Raw data often contains noise, inconsistencies, and redundancies, which can hinder accurate analysis and machine learning model performance. Data preprocessing ensures that datasets are clean, well-structured, and ready for further exploration. This chapter provides a deep dive into understanding different types of data, the structure of datasets, and essential preprocessing techniques that enhance data quality.

7.2 Understanding Data

7.2.1 Types of Data: Structured and Unstructured

Data can be broadly classified into two categories based on its organization and format: structured and unstructured data.

Structured data is highly organized and stored in a predefined schema, such as relational databases, spreadsheets, and data warehouses. It is easy to access and process using SQL queries and traditional database management systems. Examples include customer records in a CRM system containing name, email, and purchase history, employee data stored in a database with attributes such as ID, salary, and department, and financial transactions recorded in a ledger. Structured data is organized into rows and columns, can be easily queried using relational database languages like SQL, and is stored in relational databases such as MySQL, PostgreSQL, or Microsoft SQL Server.

Unstructured data lacks a predefined format, making it more challenging to store, search, and analyze. This type of data is typically found in multimedia files, social media feeds, and open-ended text responses. Examples include text documents such as emails, PDFs, and books, multimedia content like images, videos, and audio recordings, social media posts including tweets, comments, and blogs, and sensor data from IoT devices. Unstructured data has no fixed structure or organization, cannot be stored in traditional relational databases, and requires advanced processing techniques such as Natural Language Processing (NLP) for text analysis or Convolutional Neural Networks (CNNs) for image processing.

7.3 Introduction to Datasets and Their Components

A dataset is a structured collection of related data points, typically stored in a table format or as large files for processing. Each dataset contains different components that define its structure and usability.

Attributes, also known as features or variables, are columns in a dataset that represent different aspects of the data. Records, or instances, are rows in the dataset representing individual observations. The target variable, or label, is the output variable that a model aims to predict in supervised learning. Missing values are data points that are absent due to various reasons such as sensor failures or human error. Outliers are extreme values that differ significantly from the majority of the dataset. Metadata provides descriptive information about the dataset, including column names, data types, and sources.

For example, consider a dataset of customer transactions containing attributes such as Customer ID, Name, Age, Gender, Purchase Amount, and Membership Type. In this dataset, if a customer's Purchase Amount has a missing value, it must be addressed during preprocessing.

7.3.1 Data Preprocessing Techniques

Data preprocessing is a critical step in preparing raw data for analysis and machine learning. It includes data cleaning, transformation, and feature selection.

7.3.2 Handling Missing Data

Missing values can introduce bias or reduce the predictive power of models. Common strategies to address missing data include deletion, where rows or columns with excessive missing values are removed, and imputation, which replaces missing values using methods such as mean, median, or mode for numerical data, the most frequent category for categorical data, or predictive modeling techniques like k-NN or regression.

7.3.3 Handling Outliers

Outliers can distort analysis and affect model performance. Methods to detect and handle outliers include the Z-score method, which identifies values beyond three standard deviations from the mean, and the IQR (Interquartile Range) method, which considers values outside 1.5 times the IQR as outliers. Winsorization is another approach that caps extreme values to a predefined percentile.

7.3.4 Data Transformation

Transforming data can improve interpretability and model performance. Normalization, also known as Min-Max Scaling, rescales values to a fixed range, such as [0,1]. Standardization, or Z-score Scaling, converts data to have zero mean and unit variance. Log transformation is used to reduce skewness in distributions.

7.3.5 Encoding Categorical Variables

Machine learning models work with numerical data, so categorical variables need conversion. One-hot encoding converts categorical values into binary columns, while label encoding assigns integer values to categories.

7.4 Feature Engineering and Selection

Feature engineering involves creating new meaningful features from existing data, such as extracting Year of Birth from Age. Feature selection reduces dimensionality using techniques like Principal Component Analysis (PCA) or correlation analysis.

Real-World Example: Data Preprocessing in a Machine Learning Project

Consider a retail company that wants to predict customer churn using historical transaction data. The preprocessing steps include loading the dataset by reading data from a CSV file or database, handling missing values by imputing the missing Purchase Amount with the median value, detecting and removing outliers using the IQR method on Purchase Amount, converting categorical features such as Gender and

Membership Type using one-hot encoding, scaling numerical features like Age and Purchase Amount through normalization, and splitting the dataset into 80% training and 20% testing sets for model training and evaluation.

7.5 Conclusion

Data handling and preprocessing are crucial for obtaining clean and structured datasets, ensuring that analyses and machine learning models produce accurate and reliable results. By understanding different types of data, dataset components, and preprocessing techniques, one can effectively manage real-world data challenges. Properly preprocessed data not only improves model performance but also enhances interpretability, leading to better decision-making and insights.

BASIC ARTIFICIAL INTELLIGENCE SKILLS

Questions with Solutions

Q1. What is the main difference between structured and unstructured data?

Solution: Structured data is organized in a predefined schema, such as relational databases with rows and columns. Unstructured data lacks a fixed format and includes multimedia files, social media feeds, and text documents.

Q2. How can missing values be handled in a dataset?

Solution: Missing values can be handled by deletion (removing affected rows or columns) or imputation (replacing with mean, median, mode, or using predictive modeling techniques).

Q3. What is the purpose of data normalization?

Solution: Data normalization scales numerical features to a fixed range (e.g., [0,1]) to ensure uniformity and improve model performance.

Q4. What are some common methods for detecting outliers?

Solution: The Z-score method (values beyond 3 standard deviations) and the Interquartile Range (IQR) method (values outside 1.5×IQR) are commonly used for outlier detection.

Q5. Why is feature engineering important?

Solution: Feature engineering creates new, relevant features that enhance model accuracy and predictive performance by capturing useful patterns in the data.

8 DATA CLEANING AND TRANSFORMATION

8.1 Introduction

Data is the foundation of any analytical or machine learning project, but raw data is often incomplete, inconsistent, or redundant. Cleaning and transforming data ensure that it is of high quality, making it suitable for analysis and modeling. This chapter explores various data cleaning techniques, including handling missing values and duplicates, and covers transformation methods such as normalization, scaling, and encoding.

8.2 Handling Missing Values

8.2.1 Understanding Missing Data

Missing data occurs when values in a dataset are absent due

to various reasons such as human error, sensor failures, or data entry issues. If not handled properly, missing data can lead to inaccurate results and biased models.

Types of Missing Data:

Missing Completely at Random (MCAR): Data is missing without any pattern, such as a survey respondent forgetting to answer a question.

Missing at Random (MAR): Missing data is related to some observed variables, such as older participants in a survey being less likely to provide their email addresses.

Missing Not at Random (MNAR): Data is missing due to unknown reasons, such as people with lower incomes avoiding salary-related questions.

8.2.2 Strategies for Handling Missing Data

Deletion Methods:

Listwise deletion removes entire rows where any value is missing.

Column deletion drops features with excessive missing values.

Imputation Methods:

Mean, median, or mode imputation replaces missing numerical values with a calculated statistic.

Forward or backward fill uses previous or next values to fill missing data.

K-Nearest Neighbors (KNN) imputation estimates missing values based on similar instances.

Regression imputation uses regression models to predict missing values.

8.2.3 Handling Duplicates

Causes of Duplicate Data

- Data entry errors.

- Merging datasets from multiple sources.

- Web scraping and data extraction.

8.2.4 Identifying and Removing Duplicates

Detecting duplicates can be done using methods that identify repeated rows.

Removing duplicates ensures unique records are maintained in the dataset.

8.3 Data Transformation

Data transformation converts raw data into a suitable format for analysis, improving its interpretability and compatibility with machine learning models.

8.3.1 Normalization and Scaling

Scaling is essential when working with features that have varying ranges, ensuring that no single feature dominates others in the analysis.

Min-Max Scaling (Normalization):

Rescales data to a fixed range, usually between 0 and 1.

This method is useful for algorithms like neural networks and k-NN.

Z-Score Standardization:

Centers data around zero with a unit variance.

This approach is useful for distance-based models such as SVM, PCA, and K-means clustering.

Robust Scaling:

Uses median and interquartile range (IQR), making it robust to outliers.

8.3.2 Encoding Categorical Variables

Machine learning models require numerical input, so categorical data must be converted into numerical representations.

One-Hot Encoding:

Converts categorical values into binary vectors.

Each category is represented as a separate binary feature.

Label Encoding:

Assigns numerical values to categorical labels.

This method is useful when categorical values have no intrinsic ordering.

Ordinal Encoding:

Used for categories with a natural order, such as Low, Medium, and High, which are mapped to numerical values.

Binary Encoding:

Converts categories into binary code, reducing dimensionality while preserving some categorical information.

8.4 Data Cleaning and Transformation in Python

Here's a practical implementation using Python's pandas and scikit-learn:

```
import pandas as pd
import numpy as np
from sklearn.preprocessing import MinMaxScaler,
StandardScaler, OneHotEncoder

# Sample dataset
data = {'Name': ['Alice', 'Bob', 'Charlie', 'David', np.nan],
    'Age': [25, np.nan, 30, 22, 28],
    'Gender': ['Female', 'Male', 'Male', np.nan, 'Female'],
    'Salary': [50000, 54000, 60000, 58000, np.nan]}

# Create DataFrame
df = pd.DataFrame(data)

# Handling Missing Values
df['Age'].fillna(df['Age'].median(), inplace=True)      #
Median Imputation
df['Salary'].fillna(df['Salary'].mean(), inplace=True)      #
Mean Imputation
df.dropna(subset=['Gender'], inplace=True)      # Drop
missing Gender values

# Removing Duplicates
df.drop_duplicates(inplace=True)

# Normalization
scaler = MinMaxScaler()
```

```
df[['Age',   'Salary']]   =   scaler.fit_transform(df[['Age',
'Salary']])

# One-Hot Encoding
ohe = OneHotEncoder(sparse=False)
gender_encoded = ohe.fit_transform(df[['Gender']])

df_encoded   =   pd.DataFrame(gender_encoded,
columns=ohe.get_feature_names_out())
df   =   pd.concat([df,   df_encoded],
axis=1).drop(columns=['Gender'])

print(df)
```

8.5 Conclusion

Data cleaning and transformation are essential steps in ensuring high-quality datasets for analysis and machine learning. Handling missing values, removing duplicates, normalizing numerical features, and encoding categorical variables help improve the accuracy and performance of predictive models. Mastering these techniques ensures efficient and effective data-driven decision-making.

BASIC ARTIFICIAL INTELLIGENCE SKILLS

Questions with Solutions

1. Handling Missing Values

Q1: Explain the different types of missing data with examples.

Solution:
Missing data can be categorized into three types:

Missing Completely at Random (MCAR): The missing data has no relationship with any other variables. Example: A respondent in a survey forgets to answer a question.

Missing at Random (MAR): The missing data is related to some observed variables. Example: Older participants in a survey are less likely to provide their email addresses.

Missing Not at Random (MNAR): The missing data is due to an unknown pattern. Example: People with lower incomes avoiding salary-related questions in a survey.

Q2: What are the different strategies for handling missing values? Implement mean imputation for missing values in a pandas DataFrame.

Solution:
Strategies for handling missing values include:

Deletion Methods: Listwise deletion (removing rows with missing values) and column deletion.

Imputation Methods: Mean, median, mode imputation, forward/backward fill, KNN imputation, and regression imputation.

73

Python implementation of mean imputation:

```
import pandas as pd
import numpy as np

# Creating a DataFrame with missing values
data = {'Age': [25, np.nan, 30, 22, 28],
        'Salary': [50000, 54000, 60000, 58000, np.nan]}
df = pd.DataFrame(data)

# Mean Imputation
df['Salary'].fillna(df['Salary'].mean(), inplace=True)
print(df)
```

2. Handling Duplicates

Q3: Why do duplicate records occur in a dataset? How can they be removed using pandas?

Solution:
Duplicate records occur due to:

Data entry errors.

Merging datasets from multiple sources.

Web scraping and data extraction inconsistencies.

To remove duplicates in pandas:

```
# Creating a DataFrame with duplicate values
data = {'Name': ['Alice', 'Bob', 'Charlie', 'Alice'],
        'Age': [25, 30, 30, 25]}
df = pd.DataFrame(data)

# Removing duplicates
df.drop_duplicates(inplace=True)
print(df)
```

3. Data Transformation

Q4: What is the difference between normalization and standardization?

Solution:

Normalization (Min-Max Scaling): Rescales data to a fixed range (0 to 1). Useful for k-NN and neural networks.

Standardization (Z-Score Scaling): Centers data around zero with a unit variance. Useful for distance-based models such as SVM and K-means.

Q5: Implement Min-Max scaling on a numerical column in pandas using scikit-learn.

Solution:

```
from sklearn.preprocessing import MinMaxScaler


# Sample data
data = {'Age': [25, 30, 35, 40, 45]}
df = pd.DataFrame(data)


# Applying Min-Max Scaling
scaler = MinMaxScaler()
df['Age'] = scaler.fit_transform(df[['Age']])
print(df)
```

4. Encoding Categorical Variables

Q6: What are the different methods of encoding categorical variables?

Solution:

One-Hot Encoding: Converts categorical values into binary vectors.

Label Encoding: Assigns numerical values to categories.

Ordinal Encoding: Used for categories with a natural order.

Binary Encoding: Converts categories into binary code.

Q7: Implement One-Hot Encoding on a categorical column using pandas and scikit-learn.

Solution:

```
from sklearn.preprocessing import OneHotEncoder

# Sample DataFrame
data = {'Gender': ['Male', 'Female', 'Female', 'Male']}
df = pd.DataFrame(data)

# One-Hot Encoding
ohe = OneHotEncoder(sparse=False)
gender_encoded = ohe.fit_transform(df[['Gender']])
df_encoded       =       pd.DataFrame(gender_encoded,
columns=ohe.get_feature_names_out())

# Concatenating the encoded columns
df          =          pd.concat([df,          df_encoded],
axis=1).drop(columns=['Gender'])
print(df)
```

9 INTRODUCTION TO DATA VISUALIZATION

9.1 Understanding Data Visualization

Data visualization is the graphical representation of data that helps in understanding trends, patterns, and insights effectively. Instead of analyzing raw numbers, visual representations like charts, graphs, and plots make data easier to interpret.

Visualization plays a crucial role in data analysis, business intelligence, and scientific research. It helps in identifying correlations, detecting anomalies, and making informed decisions.

9.2 Basics of Data Visualization
9.2.1 Common Types of Data Visualizations
Line Chart
A line chart is used to display data points connected by straight lines. It is helpful in tracking changes over time, such as stock prices, temperature variations, and sales trends.

Bar Chart
A bar chart represents categorical data using rectangular bars. The height or length of each bar corresponds to a value, making it useful for comparing different categories.

Pie Chart
A pie chart is a circular graph divided into slices, where each slice represents a proportion of the whole dataset. It is commonly used for displaying percentage distributions.

Scatter Plot
A scatter plot uses points to represent values from two variables. It is often used in statistical analysis to determine relationships between variables.

Histogram
A histogram is a graphical representation of the distribution of numerical data. It consists of bars representing frequency distributions.

9.3 Implementing Data Visualization in C and Java
9.3.1 Line Chart Implementation
In C, we can use ASCII characters to represent a simple line chart.

C Code for Line Chart

```
#include <stdio.h>

void drawLineChart(int data[], int size) {
    for (int i = 0; i < size; i++) {
```

```c
    printf("%2d | ", data[i]);
    for (int j = 0; j < data[i]; j++) {
        printf("*");
    }
    printf("\n");
    }
}

int main() {
    int salesData[] = {3, 5, 7, 2, 6, 4, 8};
    int size = sizeof(salesData) / sizeof(salesData[0]);

    printf("Line Chart Representation:\n");
    drawLineChart(salesData, size);

    return 0;
}
```
This program prints an ASCII-based line chart where stars represent data points.

Java Code for Line Chart

```java
public class LineChart {
    public static void drawLineChart(int[] data) {
        for (int value : data) {
            System.out.print(value + " | ");
            for (int i = 0; i < value; i++) {
                System.out.print("*");
            }
            System.out.println();
        }
    }

    public static void main(String[] args) {
        int[] salesData = {3, 5, 7, 2, 6, 4, 8};

        System.out.println("Line Chart Representation:");
        drawLineChart(salesData);
```

```
   }
}
```

9.3.2 Bar Chart Implementation

A bar chart can also be created using ASCII characters.

C Code for Bar Chart

```c
#include <stdio.h>

void drawBarChart(int data[], int size) {
    for (int i = 0; i < size; i++) {
        printf("Category %d: ", i + 1);
        for (int j = 0; j < data[i]; j++) {
            printf("#");
        }
        printf("\n");
    }
}

int main() {
    int categories[] = {4, 7, 1, 8, 5, 3};
    int size = sizeof(categories) / sizeof(categories[0]);

    printf("Bar Chart Representation:\n");
    drawBarChart(categories, size);

    return 0;
}
```

Java Code for Bar Chart

```java
public class BarChart {
    public static void drawBarChart(int[] data) {
        for (int i = 0; i < data.length; i++) {
            System.out.print("Category " + (i + 1) + ": ");
            for (int j = 0; j < data[i]; j++) {
                System.out.print("#");
            }
```

```java
        System.out.println();
      }
   }

   public static void main(String[] args) {
      int[] categories = {4, 7, 1, 8, 5, 3};

      System.out.println("Bar Chart Representation:");
      drawBarChart(categories);
   }
}
```

9.3.3 Pie Chart Representation

A textual representation of a pie chart can be created by displaying percentages.

C Code for Pie Chart

```c
#include <stdio.h>

void drawPieChart(int data[], int size) {
   int total = 0;

   for (int i = 0; i < size; i++) {
      total += data[i];
   }

   printf("Pie Chart Representation:\n");
   for (int i = 0; i < size; i++) {
      printf("Category %d: %.2f%%\n", i + 1, (data[i] /
(float)total) * 100);
   }
}

int main() {
   int values[] = {10, 20, 30, 40};
   int size = sizeof(values) / sizeof(values[0]);
```

```
    drawPieChart(values, size);

    return 0;
}
```

Java Code for Pie Chart

```java
public class PieChart {
    public static void drawPieChart(int[] data) {
        int total = 0;

        for (int value : data) {
            total += value;
        }

        System.out.println("Pie Chart Representation:");
        for (int i = 0; i < data.length; i++) {
            double percentage = (data[i] / (double) total) * 100;
            System.out.printf("Category %d: %.2f%%\n", i +
1, percentage);
        }
    }

    public static void main(String[] args) {
        int[] values = {10, 20, 30, 40};

        drawPieChart(values);
    }
}
```

9.4 Key Takeaways

Line charts are useful for showing trends over time.
Bar charts are effective in comparing different categories.
Pie charts illustrate proportions within a dataset.
ASCII-based visualizations can provide a basic yet useful way to represent data in command-line applications.
While C and Java do not have built-in libraries for graphical visualization like Python's Matplotlib, they can still generate

meaningful text-based representations. More advanced visualization in Java can be done using JavaFX or Swing, and in C using graphics.h.

9.5 Conclusion

Data visualization transforms raw data into meaningful visual insights. Understanding different chart types and their implementations in programming languages helps in better decision-making. This chapter introduced basic visualizations using C and Java, demonstrating how data can be represented textually for clarity. For graphical interfaces, further exploration into external libraries and frameworks can be beneficial.

BASIC ARTIFICIAL INTELLIGENCE SKILLS

Questions with Solutions

1. Conceptual Questions
Q1. Why is data visualization important in data analysis?

Solution:
Data visualization is important because it helps in identifying patterns, trends, and insights in data. It simplifies complex datasets and makes them more understandable for decision-making, statistical analysis, and business intelligence.

Q2. What are the key differences between a bar chart and a histogram?
Solution:
Bar Chart: Represents categorical data using bars of different heights or lengths. It is used to compare discrete categories.
Histogram: Represents numerical data distributions by dividing data into bins and showing frequencies. It is used to visualize the distribution of continuous data.

Q3. What are some common types of charts used in data visualization?
Solution:
Some common types of charts include:
Line Chart: Shows trends over time.
Bar Chart: Compares categorical data.
Pie Chart: Represents data as proportional slices.
Scatter Plot: Displays relationships between two variables.
Histogram: Represents data distribution.

Q4. How can data visualization be implemented in a text-based format using C or Java?
Solution:
Data visualization can be implemented using ASCII characters like *, #, or - in the console. By iterating through data points and printing corresponding symbols, simple charts can be generated in both C and Java.

2. Coding Questions

Q5. Implement a function in C that prints a simple vertical bar chart for an array of integers.
Solution (C Code):

```c
#include <stdio.h>

void drawVerticalBarChart(int data[], int size) {
   int max = data[0];

   // Find maximum value for scaling
   for (int i = 1; i < size; i++) {
     if (data[i] > max) {
        max = data[i];
     }
   }

   // Print vertical bars
   for (int i = max; i > 0; i--) {
     for (int j = 0; j < size; j++) {
        if (data[j] >= i) {
           printf(" * ");
        } else {
           printf("   ");
        }
     }
     printf("\n");
   }

   // Print labels
   for (int i = 0; i < size; i++) {
     printf("---- ");
   }
   printf("\n");
   for (int i = 0; i < size; i++) {
     printf("%3d ", data[i]);
```

```
    }
    printf("\n");
}

int main() {
    int values[] = {3, 6, 9, 2, 8, 5};
    int size = sizeof(values) / sizeof(values[0]);

    printf("Vertical Bar Chart Representation:\n");
    drawVerticalBarChart(values, size);

    return 0;
}
```
Expected Output:

```
*
*   *
*   * *
*   * *
* * * *
* * * *
------------------
3  6  9  2  8  5
```

Q6. Write a Java program that prints a simple ASCII-based horizontal bar chart from an integer array.
Solution (Java Code):

```
public class HorizontalBarChart {
    public static void drawBarChart(int[] data) {
        for (int i = 0; i < data.length; i++) {
            System.out.print("Value " + data[i] + ": ");
            for (int j = 0; j < data[i]; j++) {
                System.out.print("#");
            }
            System.out.println();
        }
    }
```

```java
public static void main(String[] args) {
    int[] values = {5, 3, 8, 2, 6, 4};

    System.out.println("Horizontal         Bar         Chart
Representation:");
    drawBarChart(values);
  }
}
```

Expected Output:

Horizontal Bar Chart Representation:
Value 5: #####
Value 3: ###
Value 8: ########
Value 2: ##
Value 6: ######
Value 4: ####

Q7. Modify the C program for a pie chart so that it displays the percentage contribution of each category with a simple text representation.
Solution (C Code):

```c
#include <stdio.h>

void drawPieChart(int data[], int size) {
    int total = 0;

    // Calculate the total sum
    for (int i = 0; i < size; i++) {
        total += data[i];
    }

    // Print pie chart percentages
    printf("Pie Chart Representation:\n");
    for (int i = 0; i < size; i++) {
        float percentage = (data[i] / (float)total) * 100;
```

```
    printf("Category %d: %.2f%% ", i + 1, percentage);

    // Simple text representation
    for (int j = 0; j < (int)(percentage / 2); j++) {
        printf("*");
    }
    printf("\n");
    }
}

int main() {
    int values[] = {15, 25, 35, 25};
    int size = sizeof(values) / sizeof(values[0]);

    drawPieChart(values, size);

    return 0;
}
```

Expected Output:

```
Pie Chart Representation:
Category 1: 15.00% *****
Category 2: 25.00% *********
Category 3: 35.00% **************
Category 4: 25.00% *********
```

Q8. Modify the Java program to print a scatter plot where stars (*) represent points on a coordinate system.
Solution (Java Code):

```
public class ScatterPlot {
    public static void drawScatterPlot(int[] x, int[] y) {
        int maxX = 10;
        int maxY = 10;

        System.out.println("Scatter Plot Representation:");

        for (int i = maxY; i >= 0; i--) {
```

```
    for (int j = 0; j <= maxX; j++) {
        boolean found = false;
        for (int k = 0; k < x.length; k++) {
            if (x[k] == j && y[k] == i) {
                found = true;
                break;
            }
        }
        if (found) {
            System.out.print(" * ");
        } else {
            System.out.print(" . ");
        }
    }
    System.out.println();
    }
}

    public static void main(String[] args) {
        int[] x = {2, 5, 8, 1, 7};
        int[] y = {3, 6, 2, 9, 5};

        drawScatterPlot(x, y);
    }
}
```

Expected Output:

Scatter Plot Representation:

```
. . . . . . . . . .
. * . . . . . . . .
. . . . . . . . * .
. . * . . . . . . .
. . . . . . . . . .
. . . . . * . . . .
. . . . . . . . . .
. . . . . . . . . .
. . . . . . . . . .
. * . . . . . . . .
```

10 LOGICAL THINKING AND PROBLEM-SOLVING

10.1 Introduction

Logical thinking and problem-solving are fundamental skills that transcend disciplines, from mathematics and computer science to business and daily decision-making. These skills help individuals analyze situations, break them down into manageable parts, and develop systematic approaches to solving problems. A structured way of thinking not only enhances efficiency but also fosters creativity in generating solutions. In this chapter, we will explore algorithmic thinking as a subset of logical reasoning and its application in problem-solving.

10.2 Algorithmic Thinking: The Foundation of Logical Problem-Solving

Algorithmic thinking involves structuring problems into a logical sequence of steps that lead to a solution. This process is particularly essential in computing, engineering, and mathematics, where efficiency and accuracy are critical. By developing an algorithmic approach, one can tackle complex problems in a systematic manner.

10.3 Breaking Down Problems into Smaller Steps

One of the core tenets of algorithmic thinking is decomposition, which involves dividing a complex problem into smaller, more manageable sub-problems. This technique is crucial because it simplifies problem-solving by allowing individuals to focus on one aspect of the issue at a time.

10.3.1 Steps in Problem Decomposition

Identify the main problem: Clearly define the problem statement and understand the objectives.

Break it into sub-problems: Divide the problem into logical components or stages.

Analyze each component: Examine each sub-problem independently to determine its requirements and potential solutions.

Solve sub-problems individually: Implement solutions for each component before integrating them.

Integrate and refine: Combine the sub-solutions into a cohesive final solution and optimize for efficiency.

For example, consider the problem of developing a system for online food ordering. Instead of tackling the entire problem at once, one can break it down into:

- User authentication and registration

- Menu browsing and selection

- Order placement and confirmation

- Payment processing

- Order tracking and delivery

Each of these components can then be analyzed and solved separately before being integrated into a functional system.

10.4 Writing Pseudocode for Basic Algorithms

Pseudocode is a high-level representation of an algorithm that combines elements of natural language and programming constructs. It serves as an intermediary step before coding an actual program, ensuring clarity and logical correctness.

10.4.1 Basic Structure of Pseudocode

Define the input and output: Specify what data the algorithm will receive and what it should produce.

Determine the processing steps: Break down the problem into a sequence of logical steps.

Use control structures: Incorporate loops, conditionals, and function calls to guide the process flow.

Example: Finding the Largest Number in a List

```
BEGIN
    DEFINE list of numbers
    SET largest to first number in list
```

```
    FOR each number in list
        IF number > largest THEN
            SET largest to number
        END IF
    END FOR
    RETURN largest
END
```

This algorithm iterates through the list, comparing each number to the current largest value and updating it accordingly.

10.4.2 Activity: Designing an Algorithm to Solve a Real-World Problem

To reinforce the concepts discussed, let us design an algorithm for a practical scenario.

Problem Statement: Automated Traffic Light System

A city wants to implement an automated traffic light system that adapts to traffic density in real-time. The system must:

- Detect vehicle count at an intersection.

- Adjust the duration of red, yellow, and green lights accordingly.

- Ensure pedestrian safety.

Algorithm Design (Pseudocode)

```
BEGIN
    WHILE system is active
        READ vehicle count at each direction
        IF traffic is high in a direction THEN
            SET green light duration longer for that direction
        ELSE
```

```
      SET standard green light duration
    END IF
    DISPLAY yellow light for 3 seconds
    SWITCH to red light
  END WHILE
END
```

This approach ensures an adaptive traffic management system that optimizes flow based on real-time data.

10.5 Conclusion

Logical and algorithmic thinking is at the core of problem-solving. By breaking problems into smaller steps, structuring solutions using pseudocode, and designing efficient algorithms, individuals can approach complex issues systematically. Whether applied in computing, engineering, or everyday decision-making, these skills help enhance efficiency, accuracy, and innovation.

BASIC ARTIFICIAL INTELLIGENCE SKILLS

Questions with Solutions

Question 1: Sorting an Array

Problem: Write an algorithm to sort an array of integers in ascending order using the Bubble Sort technique.

Solution (Pseudocode):

```
BEGIN
  DEFINE array of numbers
  SET n to length of array
  FOR i from 0 to n-1
    FOR j from 0 to n-i-1
      IF array[j] > array[j+1] THEN
        SWAP array[j] and array[j+1]
      END IF
    END FOR
  END FOR
  RETURN array
END
```

Question 2: Finding Factorial of a Number

Problem: Write an algorithm to compute the factorial of a given number.

Solution (Pseudocode):

```
BEGIN
  FUNCTION factorial(n)
    IF n == 0 THEN
      RETURN 1
    ELSE
      RETURN n * factorial(n-1)
    END IF
  END FUNCTION
END
```

Question 3: Checking for Palindrome

Problem: Write an algorithm to check if a given string is a palindrome.

Solution (Pseudocode):

```
BEGIN
  FUNCTION isPalindrome(string)
    SET left to 0
    SET right to length of string - 1
    WHILE left < right
      IF string[left] != string[right] THEN
        RETURN false
      END IF
      INCREMENT left
      DECREMENT right
    END WHILE
    RETURN true
  END FUNCTION
END
```

Question 4: Finding the GCD of Two Numbers

Problem: Write an algorithm to find the Greatest Common Divisor (GCD) of two numbers using the Euclidean Algorithm.

Solution (Pseudocode):

```
BEGIN
  FUNCTION GCD(a, b)
    WHILE b != 0
      SET temp to b
      SET b to a MOD b
      SET a to temp
    END WHILE
```

```
    RETURN a
  END FUNCTION
END
```

11 INTRODUCTION TO DATA STRUCTURES

11.1 Understanding Data Structures

Data structures are fundamental components of computer science that allow efficient organization, storage, and manipulation of data. They provide a systematic way to manage and access data for various computational tasks. Understanding data structures is crucial for developing optimized algorithms and efficient software applications.

The choice of a data structure depends on the problem being solved, the operations that need to be performed, and the constraints on time and space complexity. In this chapter, we will explore the foundational data structures: arrays and lists, as well as basic search and sort algorithms. Additionally, we will implement a sorting algorithm using the C programming language.

11.2 Arrays: The Foundation of Data Storage

An array is a fixed-size, contiguous memory location that stores elements of the same data type. It provides fast access to elements using an index.

11.2.1 Characteristics of Arrays

Fixed size: The size of the array is determined at the time of declaration and cannot be changed dynamically.

Indexed access: Elements can be accessed using an index, providing $O(1)$ time complexity for retrieval.

Homogeneous elements: All elements must be of the same data type.

Contiguous memory allocation: Data is stored in a sequential block of memory, improving cache performance.

11.2.2 Basic Operations on Arrays

1. Insertion

Inserting an element at a specific position requires shifting elements, leading to $O(n)$ time complexity in the worst case.

2. Deletion

Deleting an element involves shifting the subsequent elements, making it an $O(n)$ operation.

3. Accessing Elements

Elements can be accessed directly using their index, with O(1) time complexity.

4. Traversal

Iterating over an array requires visiting each element, resulting in O(n) time complexity.

5. Searching

Searching for an element can be performed using linear search (O(n)) or binary search (O(log n)) if the array is sorted.

Example of Array Declaration in C

```
#include <stdio.h>

int main() {
    int numbers[5] = {10, 20, 30, 40, 50};
    printf("Element at index 2: %d\n", numbers[2]);
    return 0;
}
```

11.3 Lists: Dynamic Data Storage

Unlike arrays, lists are dynamic data structures that can grow or shrink as needed. They provide flexibility in memory usage.

11.3.1 Types of Lists

Singly Linked List: Each node contains data and a pointer to the next node.

Doubly Linked List: Each node has two pointers—one to the previous node and another to the next.

Circular Linked List: The last node points back to the first node, forming a circular structure.

11.3.2 Basic Operations on Lists

Insertion: Adding a node at the beginning, end, or middle.

Deletion: Removing a node by updating pointers.

Traversal: Moving through nodes from head to tail.

Example of a Singly Linked List Node in C

```
struct Node {
    int data;
    struct Node* next;
};
```

11.4 Simple Search Algorithms

11.4.1 Linear Search (O(n))

A simple method that scans the array sequentially.

```
int linearSearch(int arr[], int n, int key) {
    for (int i = 0; i < n; i++) {
        if (arr[i] == key) {
            return i; // Found at index i
        }
    }
    return -1; // Not found
}
```

11.4.2 Binary Search (O(log n))

Efficient search algorithm applicable to sorted arrays.

```
int binarySearch(int arr[], int left, int right, int key) {
    while (left <= right) {
        int mid = left + (right - left) / 2;
```

```
      if (arr[mid] == key)
         return mid;
      if (arr[mid] < key)
         left = mid + 1;
      else
         right = mid - 1;
   }
   return -1;
}
```

11.5 Sorting Algorithms

11.5.1 Bubble Sort

A simple sorting algorithm that repeatedly swaps adjacent elements if they are in the wrong order.

```
void bubbleSort(int arr[], int n) {
   for (int i = 0; i < n - 1; i++) {
      for (int j = 0; j < n - i - 1; j++) {
         if (arr[j] > arr[j + 1]) {
            int temp = arr[j];
            arr[j] = arr[j + 1];
            arr[j + 1] = temp;
         }
      }
   }
}
```

11.5.2 Selection Sort

Selects the smallest element and places it in the sorted portion.

```
void selectionSort(int arr[], int n) {
   for (int i = 0; i < n - 1; i++) {
      int minIdx = i;
      for (int j = i + 1; j < n; j++) {
         if (arr[j] < arr[minIdx]) {
```

```
            minIdx = j;
        }
    }
    int temp = arr[minIdx];
    arr[minIdx] = arr[i];
    arr[i] = temp;
    }
}
```

11.6 Hands-On Practice: Implementing Sorting in C

Below is a complete program that implements Bubble Sort and prints the sorted array.

```
#include <stdio.h>

void bubbleSort(int arr[], int n) {
    for (int i = 0; i < n - 1; i++) {
        for (int j = 0; j < n - i - 1; j++) {
            if (arr[j] > arr[j + 1]) {
                int temp = arr[j];
                arr[j] = arr[j + 1];
                arr[j + 1] = temp;
            }
        }
    }
}

void printArray(int arr[], int n) {
    for (int i = 0; i < n; i++) {
        printf("%d ", arr[i]);
    }
    printf("\n");
}

int main() {
    int arr[] = {64, 34, 25, 12, 22, 11, 90};
    int n = sizeof(arr) / sizeof(arr[0]);
```

```
    bubbleSort(arr, n);
    printf("Sorted array: \n");
    printArray(arr, n);
    return 0;
}
```

11.7 Conclusion

This chapter introduced fundamental data structures like arrays and lists, their basic operations, and essential search and sorting algorithms. We also implemented a sorting algorithm in C. Understanding these concepts is crucial for efficient problem-solving and algorithm design in computer science.

BASIC ARTIFICIAL INTELLIGENCE SKILLS

Questions with Solutions

1. Conceptual Questions
Q1: What are the key differences between arrays and linked
lists?

Solution:
Arrays have a fixed size, while linked lists are dynamic.
Arrays allow direct access using an index (O(1)), while linked
lists require traversal (O(n)).
Insertion/Deletion in an array requires shifting elements
(O(n)), while in a linked list, it requires pointer manipulation
(O(1) for head/tail operations).

Q2: What are the advantages and disadvantages of using arrays
over linked lists?

Solution:
Advantages: Faster access (O(1)), better cache locality.
Disadvantages: Fixed size, expensive insertions/deletions.

Q3: Compare the time complexity of linear search and binary
search.

Solution:
Linear Search: O(n), as it scans each element.
Binary Search: O(log n), as it divides the search space in half.
Condition: Binary search requires a sorted array.

2. Code-Based Questions

Q4: Write a C program to perform binary search on a sorted
array.

Solution:

```c
#include <stdio.h>

int binarySearch(int arr[], int left, int right, int key) {
    while (left <= right) {
        int mid = left + (right - left) / 2;
        if (arr[mid] == key) return mid;
        if (arr[mid] < key) left = mid + 1;
        else right = mid - 1;
    }
    return -1;
}

int main() {
    int arr[] = {10, 20, 30, 40, 50};
    int n = sizeof(arr) / sizeof(arr[0]);
    int key = 30;
    int result = binarySearch(arr, 0, n - 1, key);
    (result == -1) ? printf("Not found") : printf("Found at index %d", result);
    return 0;
}
```

Q5: Modify the bubble sort program to sort in descending order.

Solution: Change:

```c
if (arr[j] > arr[j + 1])
```

to

```c
if (arr[j] < arr[j + 1])
```
This swaps elements only if the current one is less than the next.

12 UNDERSTANDING AI LOGIC

12.1 Introduction

Artificial Intelligence (AI) has revolutionized various domains, from healthcare and finance to manufacturing and entertainment. At its core, AI seeks to emulate human decision-making through logical reasoning and computational techniques. Understanding AI logic is fundamental to comprehending how machines process information, derive conclusions, and automate decision-making. This chapter delves into the essentials of decision-making systems, exploring rule-based logic and its pivotal role in AI.

12.2 Decision-Making Systems: An Overview

Decision-making systems in AI are designed to analyze input data, evaluate potential outcomes, and choose the most suitable action based on predefined criteria. These systems can be classified into various categories, including:

Rule-Based Systems – Systems that follow predefined logic rules.

Machine Learning Models – Systems that infer patterns and make decisions based on training data.

Expert Systems – AI-driven frameworks that mimic human expert decision-making.

Fuzzy Logic Systems – Approaches that handle uncertainty and approximate reasoning.

Neural Networks & Deep Learning Models – Advanced AI architectures that recognize patterns through multiple layers of computation.

Each of these approaches has its merits and is selected based on the complexity and nature of the problem being addressed.

12.3 Rule-Based Logic: The Foundation of AI Reasoning

Rule-based logic is one of the oldest and most transparent AI decision-making methods. It involves defining a set of rules that dictate how decisions should be made based on given inputs. These rules are typically expressed in the form of IF-THEN statements.

12.3.1 Structure of Rule-Based Logic

Rule-based logic operates using the following components:

Knowledge Base: Contains facts and rules that govern the system's decision-making process.

Inference Engine: Processes input data and applies rules to deduce conclusions.

User Interface: Enables interaction between the system and users for input and output.

12.3.2 Example of Rule-Based Logic

Consider a simple medical diagnosis system designed to determine whether a patient has a fever:

Rule 1: IF temperature > 100.4°F THEN fever = true.

Rule 2: IF fever = true AND headache = true THEN condition = "Possible Flu".

Rule 3: IF fever = true AND sore throat = true THEN condition = "Possible Infection".

Here, the system evaluates the input symptoms and applies predefined rules to suggest potential diagnoses.

12.3.3 Advantages of Rule-Based Logic

Rule-based logic offers several benefits, including:

Transparency: Decisions are explainable and easy to interpret.

Consistency: Provides reliable decision-making based on defined rules.

Ease of Implementation: Simple to develop and deploy for well-defined problems.

Debugging and Modification: Easy to update by adding or modifying rules.

12.3.4 Limitations of Rule-Based Systems

Despite its advantages, rule-based logic has some limitations:

Scalability Issues: As rules increase, the system becomes complex and harder to manage.

Lack of Learning: Unlike machine learning models, rule-based systems do not improve over time unless manually updated.

Handling Uncertainty: Struggles with ambiguous or incomplete data, requiring additional techniques like fuzzy logic for better reasoning.

12.4 Enhancing Rule-Based Systems with AI Techniques

To overcome the limitations of traditional rule-based logic, AI researchers have integrated machine learning and probabilistic reasoning. Some enhancements include:

Hybrid Rule-Based and Machine Learning Models: Combining deterministic rules with data-driven learning models for improved accuracy.

Fuzzy Logic Integration: Allowing rule-based systems to handle uncertainty by introducing degrees of truth instead of binary logic.

Knowledge Graphs and Semantic Networks: Enhancing rule representation to create more sophisticated AI reasoning models.

12.5 Applications of Rule-Based Logic in AI

Rule-based systems remain relevant in various applications, such as:

Expert Systems in Medicine: Used for diagnosis and treatment recommendations.

Fraud Detection in Banking: Identifying fraudulent transactions based on predefined rules.

Automated Customer Support: Chatbots using rule-based responses for common queries.

Industrial Automation: Controlling machinery and production processes based on operational rules.

12.6 Conclusion

Understanding AI logic is essential for building intelligent systems capable of making effective decisions. Rule-based logic, despite its simplicity, remains a cornerstone of AI decision-making, particularly in scenarios requiring explainability and reliability. By integrating modern AI techniques, rule-based systems continue to evolve, bridging the gap between human-like reasoning and computational efficiency.

Questions with Solutions

1. Conceptual Questions

Q1. Define AI logic and explain its significance in decision-making systems.

Solution:
AI logic refers to the set of computational techniques and frameworks that enable machines to process information, make decisions, and emulate human reasoning. It is significant in decision-making systems as it provides structured methods for evaluating input data, analyzing potential outcomes, and selecting optimal solutions. AI logic forms the foundation for various AI-driven applications, such as expert systems, rule-based reasoning, and machine learning models.

Q2. What are the key components of a decision-making system in AI? Provide a brief description of each.

Solution:
The key components of a decision-making system in AI include:

Rule-Based Systems – Use predefined logic rules to make decisions.
Machine Learning Models – Learn patterns from training data to predict outcomes.
Expert Systems – Mimic human expertise for specialized decision-making.
Fuzzy Logic Systems – Handle uncertainty using approximate reasoning.
Neural Networks & Deep Learning Models – Use multi-layered structures to recognize complex patterns.
Each approach is chosen based on the complexity and type of problem being solved.

Q3. What are the main advantages and limitations of rule-based logic?

Solution:

Advantages:

Transparency: The reasoning process is easy to understand.
Consistency: Provides stable decision-making based on fixed rules.
Ease of Implementation: Simple to develop and deploy.
Debugging and Modification: Easy to update with new rules.
Limitations:

Scalability Issues: Becomes difficult to manage with an increasing number of rules.
Lack of Learning: Does not improve over time like machine learning models.
Handling Uncertainty: Struggles with ambiguous or incomplete data.

2. Practical and Application-Based Questions

Q4. Consider a simple rule-based system that recommends whether a student should take an umbrella. The system follows these rules:
Rule 1: IF weather = "rainy" THEN take_umbrella = true.
Rule 2: IF weather = "cloudy" AND humidity > 80% THEN take_umbrella = true.
Rule 3: IF take_umbrella = true THEN recommendation = "Carry an umbrella."
Determine the output of the system for the following inputs:
(a) weather = "sunny", humidity = 60%
(b) weather = "cloudy", humidity = 85%
(c) weather = "rainy", humidity = 70%

Solution:
(a) weather = "sunny", humidity = 60%

No rules are triggered → recommendation = "No umbrella needed."
(b) weather = "cloudy", humidity = 85%

Rule 2 is triggered → take_umbrella = true → Rule 3 is triggered
recommendation = "Carry an umbrella."
(c) weather = "rainy", humidity = 70%

Rule 1 is triggered → take_umbrella = true → Rule 3 is triggered
recommendation = "Carry an umbrella."

Q5. Consider a medical diagnosis expert system with the following rules:
Rule 1: IF fever = true AND cough = true THEN condition = "Possible Flu".
Rule 2: IF fever = true AND rash = true THEN condition = "Possible Measles".
Rule 3: IF fever = true AND sore_throat = true THEN condition = "Possible Strep Throat".
Determine the diagnosis for the following cases:
(a) fever = true, cough = true, rash = false, sore_throat = false
(b) fever = true, cough = false, rash = true, sore_throat = false
(c) fever = true, cough = false, rash = false, sore_throat = true

Solution:
(a) fever = true, cough = true, rash = false, sore_throat = false

Rule 1 is triggered → condition = "Possible Flu".
(b) fever = true, cough = false, rash = true, sore_throat = false

Rule 2 is triggered → condition = "Possible Measles".
(c) fever = true, cough = false, rash = false, sore_throat = true

Rule 3 is triggered → condition = "Possible Strep Throat".

Q6. How can integrating machine learning enhance traditional rule-based systems?

Solution:
Machine learning can enhance rule-based systems by:

Improving Adaptability: Unlike static rule-based systems, machine learning models can learn from new data and refine decision-making over time.
Handling Complexity: Can manage complex, high-dimensional data where predefined rules become impractical.
Reducing Rule Overhead: Instead of manually defining and updating rules, ML models can automatically derive decision criteria.
Enhancing Accuracy: Machine learning models can detect hidden patterns and make probabilistic decisions, improving reliability.
Hybrid Models: Combining rule-based logic with ML techniques results in systems that benefit from both transparency and adaptability.

3. Higher-Order Thinking Questions

Q7. Why is rule-based logic still used in AI, despite the advancements in machine learning and deep learning?

Solution:
Rule-based logic remains relevant due to its transparency, explainability, and deterministic nature, which are essential for applications where:

Regulatory compliance is needed (e.g., banking, healthcare).
Human trust is critical (e.g., legal decision-making, medical diagnostics).
Predictability is required, as rule-based systems provide consistent, well-defined outputs.
Computational simplicity is preferred, especially for embedded systems with limited processing power.
Despite its limitations, rule-based logic is often integrated with

modern AI techniques to enhance its scalability and adaptability.

Q8. Explain how fuzzy logic can improve the effectiveness of rule-based systems. Provide an example.

Solution:
Fuzzy logic extends rule-based systems by allowing degrees of truth rather than binary TRUE/FALSE values. This enables the system to handle uncertainty and ambiguity better.

Example:
Consider a temperature-based rule:

Traditional Rule-Based Approach:
IF temperature > 100°F THEN high_temp = true.
IF temperature ≤ 100°F THEN high_temp = false.
This results in a rigid boundary where 99.9°F is considered normal, while 100.1°F is high.

Fuzzy Logic Approach:
IF temperature is around 100°F, THEN high_temp has a gradual truth value (e.g., 0.7 instead of 1 or 0).
This approach makes the system more flexible and realistic, improving decision-making in uncertain conditions.

13 OVERVIEW OF ARTIFICIAL INTELLIGENCE AND ITS APPLICATIONS

13.1 What is AI?

Artificial Intelligence (AI) refers to the simulation of human intelligence in machines that are programmed to think, learn, and solve problems. AI enables machines to perform tasks that typically require human intelligence, such as understanding language, recognizing patterns, making decisions, and improving through experience.

AI can be categorized into two types:

Narrow AI (Weak AI): AI systems that are designed for a specific task, such as voice assistants like Siri or Alexa, recommendation systems, and autonomous vehicles.

General AI (Strong AI): A more advanced AI that possesses human-like cognitive abilities, allowing it to understand, learn, and apply knowledge across different domains.

13.2 Definition and History of AI

The concept of artificial intelligence dates back to ancient times when myths and folklore depicted intelligent automata. However, AI as a scientific discipline began in the mid-20th century. The field has gone through various phases of progress and setbacks, known as AI "winters" and "booms."

Key Milestones in AI History:

1950: Alan Turing proposed the Turing Test to determine machine intelligence.

1956: The Dartmouth Conference marked the official birth of AI as a research field.

1960s-1970s: Early AI systems developed rule-based problem-solving and reasoning capabilities.

1980s: Introduction of expert systems and knowledge-based AI.

1990s-2000s: Machine learning, probabilistic reasoning, and neural networks gained popularity.

2010s-Present: The deep learning revolution, big data, and computational advancements fueled AI's rapid expansion across industries.

13.3 Key Areas of AI

AI comprises multiple subfields, each focusing on specific aspects of intelligence. Some of the most important areas include:

BASIC ARTIFICIAL INTELLIGENCE SKILLS

1. Machine Learning (ML)

Machine learning is a subset of AI that allows systems to learn from data and make predictions or decisions without being explicitly programmed. ML algorithms include:

- Supervised Learning: Training with labeled data (e.g., spam email detection).

- Unsupervised Learning: Finding patterns in unlabeled data (e.g., customer segmentation).

- Reinforcement Learning: Learning through rewards and penalties (e.g., AlphaGo, self-driving cars).

2. Robotics

Robotics involves the design and creation of autonomous machines capable of performing tasks in real-world environments. AI-powered robots are used in:

- Manufacturing (e.g., industrial robots in assembly lines)

- Healthcare (e.g., surgical robots, robotic prosthetics)

- Exploration (e.g., Mars rovers, deep-sea exploration robots)

3. Natural Language Processing (NLP)

NLP enables computers to understand, interpret, and respond to human language. Applications of NLP include:

- Speech Recognition: Voice assistants like Google Assistant and Siri.

- Machine Translation: Google Translate, DeepL.

- Chatbots and Virtual Assistants: AI-driven customer support bots.

4. Computer Vision

Computer vision enables machines to interpret and analyze visual data, such as images and videos. Applications include:

- Facial recognition systems

- Medical image analysis (e.g., detecting tumors in X-rays)

- Autonomous vehicles (object detection and navigation)

5. Expert Systems

Expert systems mimic human decision-making using rule-based logic and knowledge bases. They are used in:

- Medical diagnosis (e.g., AI-driven diagnostics)

- Financial analysis (e.g., fraud detection)

- Industrial automation

6. AI in Gaming

AI plays a crucial role in modern video games, enhancing player experience and creating adaptive, challenging opponents. Examples include:

- Game AI in chess and Go (e.g., AlphaGo)

- Dynamic character behaviors in video games (e.g., NPCs in open-world games)

7. Fuzzy Logic Systems

Fuzzy logic allows AI systems to handle uncertainty and approximate reasoning. Applications include:

- Automated climate control

- Consumer electronics (e.g., smart washing machines)

13.4 Applications of AI

AI is transforming numerous industries and everyday life, enabling efficiency, automation, and intelligent decision-making.

1. AI in Healthcare

- Medical Imaging: AI-driven radiology for detecting diseases.

- Drug Discovery: AI algorithms accelerating pharmaceutical research.

- Personalized Medicine: AI tailoring treatments based on genetic data.

- Robotic Surgery: AI-assisted robotic systems improving surgical precision.

2. AI in Finance

- Fraud Detection: AI analyzing transaction patterns to detect fraud.

- Algorithmic Trading: AI making high-frequency stock market decisions.

- Customer Support: AI chatbots assisting customers in banking.

3. AI in Manufacturing

- Predictive Maintenance: AI predicting equipment failures before they occur.

- Quality Control: AI-powered visual inspection in factories.

- Supply Chain Optimization: AI-driven logistics management.

4. AI in Education

- Smart Tutoring Systems: Personalized AI tutors helping students.

- Automated Grading: AI grading essays and assignments.

- Language Learning: AI-powered translation and pronunciation tools.

5. AI in Transportation

- Self-Driving Cars: AI-based autonomous vehicles reducing human error.

- Traffic Management: AI optimizing urban traffic flow.

- Route Optimization: AI-powered GPS navigation.

6. AI in Retail

- Personalized Recommendations: AI suggesting products to customers.

- Automated Inventory Management: AI optimizing stock levels.

- Checkout-Free Stores: AI-powered cashier-less shopping experiences.

7. AI in Agriculture

- Precision Farming: AI analyzing soil and crop health.

- Automated Harvesting: AI-driven robotic farming equipment.

- Pest Control: AI identifying and preventing infestations.

- Activity: Watching and Discussing Case Studies of AI Applications

To better understand AI's impact, consider analyzing real-world case studies:

Case Study 1: AI in Healthcare – IBM Watson

IBM Watson uses AI to analyze vast medical databases and assist doctors in diagnosing and treating diseases. It can process millions of medical records and suggest treatment plans based on patient data.

Discussion Points:

- How does AI improve diagnostic accuracy?

- What are the ethical concerns of AI in medicine?

- Can AI replace human doctors?

Case Study 2: AI in Finance – Fraud Detection

Financial institutions use AI to detect fraudulent transactions by analyzing spending patterns and anomalies in real time.

Discussion Points:

- How does AI identify fraud faster than humans?

- What are the limitations of AI in financial security?

Case Study 3: AI in Transportation – Tesla Autopilot

Tesla's Autopilot uses deep learning and computer vision to enable semi-autonomous driving, reducing accidents and improving driving efficiency.

Discussion Points:

- How reliable is AI in self-driving technology?

- What are the risks and ethical considerations?

13.5 Conclusion

AI is a transformative force shaping various aspects of human life. From healthcare and finance to education and transportation, AI is driving innovation and efficiency. Understanding AI's core principles, key areas, and applications allows us to appreciate its benefits and address its challenges responsibly. As AI continues to evolve, it is crucial to balance technological advancements with ethical considerations to ensure a positive impact on society.

BASIC ARTIFICIAL INTELLIGENCE SKILLS

Questions with Solutions

1. What is Artificial Intelligence (AI)?
Question: Define Artificial Intelligence and explain its significance in modern technology.

Solution:
Artificial Intelligence (AI) is the simulation of human intelligence in machines, enabling them to perform tasks that typically require human cognition, such as learning, reasoning, problem-solving, and decision-making. AI plays a crucial role in modern technology by automating processes, enhancing efficiency, and enabling innovations in various fields such as healthcare, finance, and manufacturing.

2. Describe the history of AI and its major milestones.
Question: Outline the key developments in the history of AI from its inception to modern advancements.

Solution:
1950s: Alan Turing proposed the Turing Test to assess machine intelligence.
1956: The Dartmouth Conference marked the birth of AI as a formal field of study.
1960s-1970s: Early AI programs, such as ELIZA (natural language processing) and Shakey (robotics), were developed.
1980s: Expert systems and rule-based AI gained popularity.
1990s: AI saw improvements in machine learning and computational power (e.g., IBM's Deep Blue defeating chess champion Garry Kasparov in 1997).
2000s-Present: The rise of deep learning, neural networks, and AI applications in self-driving cars, virtual assistants, and healthcare.

3. What are the key areas of Artificial Intelligence?
Question: List and briefly describe the major domains of AI.

Solution:

Machine Learning (ML): AI systems that learn from data to make predictions or decisions.

Robotics: AI-driven machines that can perform tasks autonomously.

Natural Language Processing (NLP): AI techniques that enable computers to understand, interpret, and generate human language.

Computer Vision: AI-powered image and video analysis for object recognition and pattern detection.

Expert Systems: AI that mimics human expert decision-making in fields like medicine and law.

4. Explain the concept of Machine Learning with an example.
Question: What is Machine Learning, and how does it work? Provide an example.

Solution:
Machine Learning (ML) is a subset of AI that allows computers to learn patterns from data without being explicitly programmed. It involves training algorithms on datasets to improve their accuracy over time.

Example:
A spam filter in email services is an ML model that learns from past data to classify emails as spam or non-spam based on features like sender, content, and keywords.

5. How does Natural Language Processing (NLP) work?
Question: Describe the working principles of NLP and its real-world applications.

Solution:
Natural Language Processing (NLP) enables machines to understand, analyze, and generate human language. It combines linguistics with machine learning to interpret text and speech.

Real-world applications:

Chatbots: Automated customer service (e.g., Siri, Alexa).
Language Translation: Google Translate for multilingual communication.
Text Summarization: AI tools that summarize articles and reports.

6. Activity-Based Question
Question: Watch a case study on AI applications in healthcare (e.g., IBM Watson). Discuss how AI is transforming medical diagnostics.

Solution:

AI in healthcare helps in early disease detection, drug discovery, and personalized treatment.
AI-powered systems like IBM Watson analyze medical records to suggest possible diagnoses and treatments.
Discuss ethical concerns like data privacy and algorithm biases.

14 AI IN EVERYDAY LIFE

14.1 Introduction

Artificial Intelligence (AI) is no longer a futuristic concept confined to research labs; it is seamlessly integrated into our daily lives. From waking up to an AI-powered alarm to receiving personalized recommendations on entertainment platforms, AI influences how we interact with technology, businesses, and the world. This chapter explores how AI powers search engines, chatbots, and recommendation systems, as well as its applications in industries such as healthcare, finance, and education.

14.2 AI in Everyday Digital Interactions

14.2.1 AI-Powered Search Engines

Search engines like Google, Bing, and DuckDuckGo use AI to provide relevant search results, autocomplete suggestions, and personalized search experiences. The backbone of these search engines includes:

- Natural Language Processing (NLP): Understanding search queries in human language.

- Machine Learning Algorithms: Learning from user behavior to rank search results effectively.

- AI-Driven Indexing: Crawling and categorizing vast amounts of data for quick retrieval.

- Voice Search & Assistants: Google Assistant, Siri, and Alexa use AI to understand voice commands and provide accurate answers.

14.2.2 AI Chatbots and Virtual Assistants

Chatbots and virtual assistants like ChatGPT, Apple's Siri, and Amazon Alexa have revolutionized communication by handling customer inquiries, booking appointments, and even assisting in therapy sessions. Their key technologies include:

- Conversational AI: Understanding and responding to human queries in a meaningful way.

- Deep Learning Models: Improving accuracy over time by analyzing vast amounts of interaction data.

- Sentiment Analysis: Detecting user emotions to tailor responses.

14.2.3 AI-Powered Recommendation Systems

Recommendation systems power platforms like Netflix, YouTube, Amazon, and Spotify by analyzing user preferences to suggest content. AI enables:

- Collaborative Filtering: Suggesting content based on similar user behavior.

- Content-Based Filtering: Analyzing user interests and recommending similar items.

- Hybrid Approaches: Combining multiple AI techniques for more accurate recommendations.

14.3 AI in Key Industries

14.3.1 AI in Healthcare

AI has transformed healthcare by improving diagnostics, patient care, and medical research. Major applications include:

- AI-Powered Diagnostics: Machine learning models detecting diseases from medical images (e.g., detecting cancer in MRI scans).

- Virtual Health Assistants: Chatbots like Babylon Health provide initial medical consultations.

- Predictive Analytics: AI predicts disease outbreaks and patient deterioration using historical data.

- Robotic Surgery: AI-assisted surgical robots perform delicate operations with precision.

14.3.2 AI in Finance

The financial industry leverages AI for fraud detection, risk management, and customer service. Some common applications include:

- Algorithmic Trading: AI executes high-speed trades based on market data analysis.

- Fraud Detection: AI systems monitor transactions in real-time to detect anomalies.

- Chatbots for Banking: Virtual assistants help users manage accounts and answer queries.

- Credit Scoring & Risk Assessment: AI predicts loan default risks by analyzing financial history.

14.3.3 AI in Education

AI is reshaping education by personalizing learning experiences and automating administrative tasks. Some applications include:

- Adaptive Learning Systems: AI-powered platforms adjust coursework difficulty based on student performance (e.g., Duolingo, Coursera).

- Automated Grading: AI evaluates essays and assignments, saving educators time.

- Virtual Tutors: AI-powered tutoring systems offer assistance outside traditional classrooms.

- AI-Powered Student Analytics: Identifying at-risk students for early intervention.

14.4 Ethical Considerations and Challenges

While AI enhances convenience, it also raises ethical concerns:

- Bias in AI Algorithms: AI systems can inherit biases from training data, leading to unfair outcomes.

- Privacy Issues: AI-driven personalization requires

collecting vast amounts of user data, raising security concerns.

- Job Displacement: Automation may replace certain jobs, necessitating workforce reskilling.

- AI Decision Transparency: Black-box models make it difficult to interpret AI decisions, impacting trust and accountability.

14.5 Future of AI in Everyday Life

The future of AI in daily life is promising, with advancements in:

Smarter AI Assistants: AI becoming more context-aware and proactive in assisting users.

Enhanced Personalization: AI refining recommendations based on deeper behavioral insights.

AI for Sustainability: AI optimizing energy use, reducing waste, and promoting eco-friendly innovations.

Augmented Reality (AR) and AI Integration: AI-enhanced AR applications for education, training, and entertainment.

14.6 Conclusion

AI is deeply embedded in our daily lives, enhancing efficiency, personalization, and decision-making. From search engines and chatbots to revolutionizing healthcare, finance, and education, AI is an indispensable force driving technological progress. While challenges exist, continuous improvements and ethical AI development will shape a future where AI enriches human lives without compromising fairness and security.

BASIC ARTIFICIAL INTELLIGENCE SKILLS

Questions with Solutions

Q1: Explain how AI has become an integral part of our daily lives.

Solution: AI is embedded in various aspects of daily life, from AI-powered alarms to personalized content recommendations. It powers search engines, chatbots, and recommendation systems and is used in industries like healthcare, finance, and education to enhance efficiency, accuracy, and decision-making.

Q2: How does Natural Language Processing (NLP) help search engines like Google and Bing?

Solution: NLP enables search engines to understand search queries in human language by interpreting meaning, context, and intent. This allows for more accurate and relevant search results, even when queries are phrased conversationally.

Q3: What role does AI play in voice search and assistants like Siri and Alexa?

Solution: AI enables voice assistants to process spoken commands, understand user intent, and provide relevant responses. This is achieved using speech recognition, NLP, and machine learning techniques to improve accuracy over time.

Q4: What are the key technologies behind AI chatbots?

Solution:
Conversational AI allows chatbots to understand and respond to human queries.
Deep Learning Models improve chatbot responses by learning from previous interactions.
Sentiment Analysis helps chatbots detect user emotions and tailor responses accordingly.

Q5: How do AI-powered chatbots enhance customer service?

Solution: Chatbots provide 24/7 customer support, handle multiple queries simultaneously, offer personalized responses, and reduce response time, improving overall customer experience.

Q6: Compare collaborative filtering and content-based filtering in AI-powered recommendation systems.

Solution:
Collaborative Filtering: Recommends content based on user behavior similarities (e.g., "People who bought this also bought...").
Content-Based Filtering: Analyzes item features and user preferences to recommend similar content (e.g., suggesting movies based on past ratings).

Q7: Why do platforms like Netflix and Spotify use hybrid recommendation systems?

Solution: Hybrid systems combine collaborative and content-based filtering for better accuracy. This approach overcomes individual limitations, ensuring personalized and relevant recommendations.

Q8: How does AI improve disease diagnosis in healthcare?

Solution: AI-powered diagnostics use machine learning models to analyze medical images (e.g., X-rays, MRIs) and detect diseases like cancer early with higher accuracy than traditional methods.

Q9: What is the role of predictive analytics in healthcare?

Solution: Predictive analytics uses AI to analyze historical patient data and forecast disease outbreaks, potential health risks, and patient deterioration, allowing early intervention.

Q10: How does AI assist in fraud detection?

Solution: AI detects fraudulent transactions by analyzing patterns and anomalies in real-time. Machine learning models flag unusual activities, helping prevent financial fraud.

Q11: Explain how algorithmic trading benefits from AI.

Solution: AI processes vast amounts of market data to execute high-speed, data-driven trades. It minimizes risks and optimizes profit margins by identifying trends and making split-second trading decisions.

Q12: What are the benefits of AI-powered adaptive learning systems?

Solution: Adaptive learning platforms adjust course material difficulty based on student performance, providing a personalized learning experience. This enhances understanding and retention.

Q13: How does AI help in automated grading?

Solution: AI-powered systems evaluate multiple-choice tests, written assignments, and essays using NLP and machine learning, reducing the workload of educators and ensuring objective grading.

Q14: Why is bias in AI algorithms a concern?

Solution: AI models inherit biases from training data, which can lead to unfair outcomes, discrimination, or misrepresentation, especially in sensitive areas like hiring and law enforcement.

Q15: How does AI impact job displacement, and what can be done to address it?

Solution: AI automation may replace certain jobs, especially in repetitive tasks. To mitigate this, workforce reskilling and upskilling initiatives should be implemented to prepare workers for AI-driven roles.

Q16: What are some ways AI can contribute to sustainability?

Solution: AI can optimize energy consumption, reduce waste, and promote eco-friendly innovations, such as smart grids and AI-driven climate modeling.

Q17: How might AI enhance augmented reality (AR) applications?

Solution: AI-powered AR can improve education, training, and entertainment by providing real-time, interactive, and immersive experiences tailored to user needs.

Q18: Summarize the key impact of AI on society.

Solution: AI enhances efficiency, personalization, and decision-making across industries, from search engines and chatbots to healthcare, finance, and education. While challenges exist, ethical AI development ensures a fair and secure future.

15 PREPARING FOR ADVANCED AI STUDIES

15.1 Introduction

Artificial Intelligence (AI) is an evolving field that requires a strong foundation in mathematics, programming, and critical thinking. As AI becomes more integral to industries ranging from healthcare to finance, preparing for advanced AI studies is essential for those aspiring to contribute meaningfully to the field. This chapter provides a structured approach to understanding the prerequisites for advanced AI learning, explores the tools and resources for self-study, and presents a roadmap to transition into advanced AI courses successfully.

15.2 Understanding the Prerequisites for Advanced AI Learning

15.2.1 Mathematical Foundations

Mathematics is the backbone of AI and machine learning (ML). Before diving into advanced AI studies, one should master the following concepts:

- Linear Algebra: Understanding vectors, matrices, eigenvalues, eigenvectors, and matrix factorization techniques like Singular Value Decomposition (SVD).

- Probability and Statistics: Concepts such as Bayes' theorem, probability distributions, expectation, variance, Markov chains, and hypothesis testing are fundamental for AI models.

- Calculus: Differentiation, integration, partial derivatives, and optimization techniques like gradient descent are crucial for neural networks and deep learning.

- Discrete Mathematics: Graph theory, combinatorics, and Boolean algebra play a role in AI algorithms and data structures.

15.2.2 Programming Skills

A solid grasp of programming is required to implement AI algorithms effectively. Essential skills include:

- Python Proficiency: Python is the dominant language in AI due to its rich ecosystem of libraries such as NumPy, Pandas, TensorFlow, and PyTorch.

- Understanding of Algorithms and Data Structures: Knowledge of sorting algorithms, searching algorithms, linked lists, trees, and graphs is crucial for AI development.

- Version Control (Git & GitHub): Collaboration in AI projects often requires version control to manage code efficiently.

15.2.3 Core AI Concepts

Understanding basic AI concepts is necessary before progressing to advanced topics. These include:

- Supervised and Unsupervised Learning

- Feature Engineering and Data Preprocessing

- Model Evaluation Metrics (Precision, Recall, F1-score, ROC Curve)

- Basic Neural Networks and Backpropagation

15.2.4 Domain Knowledge

AI applications differ across industries. Having domain-specific knowledge in healthcare, finance, robotics, or NLP helps tailor AI solutions effectively.

15.3 Tools and Resources for Self-Study in AI

15.3.1 Online Courses and Certifications

Self-study in AI has never been more accessible with numerous online platforms offering courses:

- Coursera (Andrew Ng's Machine Learning, Deep Learning Specialization by DeepLearning.AI)

- edX (MIT's Introduction to AI, Harvard's Data

Science Program)

- Udacity (AI for Robotics, Deep Learning Nanodegree)

- Kaggle Courses (Free hands-on AI projects and competitions)

- Fast.ai (Practical deep learning for coders)

15.3.2 Books for Deep Understanding

Some essential books for AI learners include:

- "Pattern Recognition and Machine Learning" by Christopher Bishop

- "Deep Learning" by Ian Goodfellow, Yoshua Bengio, and Aaron Courville

- "Hands-On Machine Learning with Scikit-Learn, Keras, and TensorFlow" by Aurélien Géron

- "Artificial Intelligence: A Modern Approach" by Stuart Russell and Peter Norvig

15.3.3 Open Source Frameworks

Familiarity with AI frameworks accelerates learning. Some key tools include:

- TensorFlow & Keras: Deep learning framework for neural networks

- PyTorch: Widely used in research for its dynamic computational graph

- Scikit-learn: Essential for classical ML techniques

- OpenCV: Used for computer vision tasks

- NLTK & SpaCy: Libraries for Natural Language Processing (NLP)

15.3.4 AI Communities and Research Papers

Engagement with AI communities helps in staying updated with the latest advancements. Useful resources include:

- ArXiv & Google Scholar: Research paper repositories

- GitHub: Open-source AI projects

- Reddit (r/MachineLearning, r/artificial): Discussions on AI advancements

- Kaggle: AI competitions and discussions

15.4 Building a Roadmap to Transition to the Advanced Course

15.4.1 Step 1: Assess Current Knowledge

Before transitioning to an advanced AI course, evaluate proficiency in mathematics, programming, and AI fundamentals. Take self-assessments on platforms like Leetcode, HackerRank, or Kaggle challenges.

15.4.2 Step 2: Strengthen Weak Areas

If weak in mathematics, focus on linear algebra, statistics, and calculus.

If weak in programming, work on Python projects and AI implementations.

If unfamiliar with AI concepts, complete a few beginner-level AI projects before diving into advanced courses.

15.4.3 Step 3: Work on AI Projects

- Hands-on experience is crucial for mastering AI. Suggested projects:

- Image classification using Convolutional Neural Networks (CNNs)

- Sentiment analysis with NLP techniques

- Fraud detection using anomaly detection algorithms

- Building a recommendation system for a retail dataset

15.4.4 Step 4: Study Advanced AI Topics

Once comfortable with foundational concepts, transition to advanced topics:

- Deep Learning (GANs, Transformer models like BERT, GPT)

- Reinforcement Learning (Q-Learning, Deep Q-Networks, AlphaGo)

- Bayesian Learning and Probabilistic Graphical Models

- Explainable AI (XAI) and AI Ethics

15.4.5 Step 5: Participate in AI Research and Competitions

- Contribute to open-source AI projects.

- Publish AI research on platforms like ArXiv.

- Participate in AI competitions such as Kaggle, AI4Good, or NeurIPS challenges.

15.4.6 Step 6: Enroll in Advanced AI Courses

After covering self-study materials, consider enrolling in advanced AI courses:

- Stanford's CS231n (Deep Learning for Vision)

- MIT's Deep Learning for Self-Driving Cars

- CMU's Reinforcement Learning Course

- Harvard's Data Science and AI Ethics Program

15.5 Conclusion

Preparing for advanced AI studies requires dedication and a structured approach. By mastering foundational concepts, leveraging self-study resources, and engaging in hands-on projects, one can smoothly transition to advanced AI learning. The roadmap provided ensures a step-by-step progression from beginner to expert, ultimately preparing learners to contribute to cutting-edge AI advancements. The future of AI is dynamic and promising, and thorough preparation will ensure success in this exciting and transformative field.

BASIC ARTIFICIAL INTELLIGENCE SKILLS

Questions with Solutions

1. Understanding the Prerequisites for Advanced AI Learning
Q1: What fundamental topics should a student master before diving into advanced AI studies?

Solution: Before starting advanced AI studies, a student should be proficient in:

Mathematics: Linear Algebra, Probability, Statistics, and Calculus.
Programming: Python, libraries such as NumPy, Pandas, TensorFlow, and PyTorch.
Machine Learning Basics: Supervised and unsupervised learning, optimization techniques, evaluation metrics.
Data Handling: Data preprocessing, feature engineering, and working with large datasets.

2. Tools and Resources for Self-Study in AI
Q2: What are some recommended online resources for self-studying AI?

Solution: Several online platforms provide excellent AI learning resources:

Courses:
Coursera (Deep Learning Specialization by Andrew Ng)
Udacity (AI for Everyone, Machine Learning Engineer Nanodegree)
edX (MIT's Introduction to Deep Learning)
Books:
"Pattern Recognition and Machine Learning" by Christopher Bishop
"Deep Learning" by Ian Goodfellow
"Hands-On Machine Learning" by Aurélien Géron
Coding Platforms:
Kaggle (hands-on datasets and challenges)

Google Colab (for implementing AI models without local setup)
GitHub (for sharing and collaborating on AI projects)

3. Building a Roadmap to Transition to the Advanced Course
Q3: How can a student structure their learning path to transition from beginner to advanced AI studies?

Solution: A structured roadmap includes:

Foundation Stage:

Strengthen mathematical foundations.
Learn programming (Python, libraries like TensorFlow, Scikit-learn).
Complete beginner-friendly AI courses.
Intermediate Stage:

Implement machine learning models from scratch.
Work on real-world datasets (e.g., ImageNet, MNIST, UCI datasets).
Participate in AI competitions (e.g., Kaggle, DrivenData).
Advanced Stage:

Study deep learning architectures (CNNs, RNNs, GANs, Transformers).
Explore AI ethics and bias in models.
Research state-of-the-art AI models (BERT, GPT, Diffusion Models).
Contribute to AI research through academic papers or GitHub projects.

4. Practical Applications of AI Knowledge
Q4: Why is hands-on experience with AI projects essential, and how can students gain it?

Solution: Hands-on experience is crucial because:

It reinforces theoretical concepts through real-world application.
It builds a strong portfolio for academic and career opportunities.
It enhances problem-solving skills by working on diverse datasets.
To gain experience, students should:

Work on open-source projects: Contribute to AI-based repositories on GitHub.
Engage in AI internships: Apply for AI-related internships in companies.
Compete in hackathons: Platforms like Hackerearth and Kaggle host competitions.
Develop personal projects: Build AI models for text generation, image classification, or predictive analytics.

5. Overcoming Challenges in Advanced AI Studies
Q5: What are some common challenges students face when learning advanced AI, and how can they be overcome?

Solution:

Challenge: Difficulty in understanding complex AI algorithms.

Solution: Break problems into smaller concepts, use visualization tools like TensorBoard.
Challenge: Lack of computing resources for deep learning models.

Solution: Use cloud-based AI services like Google Colab, AWS, or Microsoft Azure.
Challenge: Keeping up with rapid AI advancements.

Solution: Follow AI research papers on arXiv, subscribe to AI newsletters, and join AI communities (Reddit ML, AI conferences).

ABOUT THE AUTHOR

Dr. Prasun Bhattacharjee is a Ph.D. in Engineering (Awarded by the Department of Mechanical Engineering of the prestigious Jadavpur University of Kolkata, India). His numerous scientific contributions have been published in distinguished peer-reviewed journals. Prasun has also presented his research works at several international conferences held in the USA and European nations. He is currently a member of the Indian Institute of Welding and the Association for Information Systems. His research mainly focuses on employing artificial intelligence techniques to enhance the performance of wind power generation systems. Dr. Bhattacharjee earned the university medal of the Maulana Abul Kalam Azad University of Technology, West Bengal while studying for the Master of Technology degree in Industrial Engineering and Management. He has also worked for the distinguished TATA group as a Systems Engineer after passing out from the Kalyani Government Engineering College as a mechanical engineer. Dr. Bhattacharjee has traveled extensively to almost every corner of India and 26 foreign nations with his parents. He loves to share his travel experiences with other fellow nomads to help them witness the wonders of the world on their own. You can enjoy his exhilarating travel videos on his YouTube channel (https://www.youtube.com/c/prasunbhattacharjee1206) or visit the author on Twitter (@Prasun6official). Dr. Bhattacharjee is presently serving as a faculty in Mechanical Engineering.

www.ingramcontent.com/pod-product-compliance
Lightning Source LLC
LaVergne TN
LVHW051239050326
832903LV00028B/2471